4.72

Goethe's Faust

AS A RENAISSANCE MAN

Goethe's Faust

AS A RENAISSANCE MAN:

PARALLELS

AND PROTOTYPES

BY HAROLD _stein_ JANTZ

PRINCETON, NEW JERSEY

PRINCETON UNIVERSITY PRESS

1951

Printed in the United States of America

by Princeton University Press at Princeton, New Jersey

TO

A. R. HOHLFELD

SCHOLAR AND TEACHER

PREFACE

N THIS INQUIRY into the Renaissance backgrounds of Goethe's *Faust* we shall be traversing unfamiliar territory toward a very familiar goal. From the new prospect even the goal will look strangely different, but such newness can be meaningful only if it opens up a further and perhaps better perspective on the great dramatic poem. I hope to show that the new approach is in agreement with Goethe's known inclinations and intentions, that in the work itself it reveals bonds of unity and harmony between seemingly discrepant parts, and that it will contribute substantially to a final comprehensive and adequate interpretation of the whole.

One readily visible advantage of the new approach is its tendency to avoid some of the chief obstacles lying along the familiar approaches to the work. Hitherto the critical expositions have been frequently afflicted with two kinds of subjectivity: an extreme biographical interpretation of the work as a self-expression of Goethe, and an over-personal reaction of the critic within the circle of his own self, time, and position. The one subjectivity furnishes far too small a platform and background for this mighty drama and cannot account for major features of it that quite obviously are there. The other subjectivity shows us more of the critic than of the work; it selects, colors, refracts, shifts, and re-emphasizes it out of all semblance to its original self. The one restricts *Faust* unduly, the other distorts it.

Sad experience has shown that a direct, unaided perusal will, ironically, lead not to a purer and truer comprehension of the poem but only to even more subjectively colored and fragmental reactions within certain limited aspects of it. Goethe's poem, like Dante's or like many another of most exalted rank, is too inclusive and manifold for immediate apperception. However, such scholarly and critical guidance as is necessary should be both adequate to its purpose and self-effacing. Might it not help then toward fullness as well as objectivity if, instead of putting an analysis of the poem *between* us and it, we rather put a broad and deep background *behind* it? Then we could look at it directly, without the refraction and discoloration of an intervening mind, and at the same time look at it in its natural and sufficient setting.

This sufficient setting, as it turns out, is not merely the background of Goethe seen personally in his immediate environment but is rather the deeper and broader background of the whole era of three centuries and more from which the work emerged and which it interprets in permanently valid poetic symbol. A study of the larger realms of art and thought from which it developed will tell us much about its intrinsic heritage of form and intent. Those thinkers who established the tradition of the ideals and attitudes and rules of life to which Faust subscribes and by which he is ultimately judged, will also help us to understand the work and its fundamental premises.

If Goethe tells us plainly and directly that he studied the fifteenth and sixteenth centuries intensively at the inception of *Faust*, we can do no better than follow him and see what he learned there. And yet, the two chief founders of the Renaissance intellectual tradition have hardly been so much as mentioned in connection with the drama. Instead, the philosophies subsequent to *Faust* (that is, between us and it) have dominated the critical approaches to the work. These philosophies (and psychologies), from Kant, Fichte, and Hegel, through Nietzsche, to the present, are often fascinating in their varied reactions to problems and phases of the drama. Such reactions, however, tell us something significant only about the philosophers and philosophies concerned; they tell us nothing reliable or decisive about *Faust* itself. It would

indeed be futile to expect them to do so; they can only re-
fract, distort, and discolor the clear, clean image of the work
by interposing themselves in the line of our vision.

Likewise the imagery and symbolism of *Faust* have their
full connotation only in the great artistic tradition out of
which they developed. When even in Goethe's lifetime the
younger generation lost understanding for this encompassing
symbolic complex and retreated, each man or clique, into a
little world of private symbolism for subjective imaginings,
the ground was lost for the natural comprehension of the
drama on its own terms. Subsequent attempts to demonstrate
its "unity" became all too often artificial constructions alien
to the nature of the poem. Only in the last thirty years or
so have scholars, chiefly in another field, recovered the lost
symbolic complex from which the work can be better comprehended poetically.

It is clear and undeniable that the century or so up to, and
beyond, 1770 contributed significantly to the moulding and
forming of *Faust*; but that the thought, art, and life of this
period are adequate to account for all or even most of the
characteristic features of the work is an assumption which
has been too lightly made, as I hope to show. An eighteenth-
century background leaves many important features of the
poem in obscurity or in doubt; obviously this great work
needs a larger background. When the drama is organically
placed in its full environment, we can readily observe that
it is not merely or chiefly the intensely personal expression
of its author, not merely the reflection of the close-knit little
circles of the literary revolution (the Storm and Stress) and
its golden Weimar transmutation, not merely the product
of the eighteenth and the prelude to the nineteenth century; rather, the work is the culminating expression and
summation of an entire era, which we are (or were) accustomed to call the Renaissance. The more extensive eras of

the Middle Ages and antiquity also give of their life to the poem, and they are decidedly not neglected in this study.

Any such new approach as this will always run the danger of being misunderstood in a variety of ways, despite the care that may be taken to lay the fundamental groundwork. In the very title, for example, the term "Renaissance Man" has almost nothing in common with the stereotyped technical term developed by the nineteenth-century historians to describe a few specimens arbitrarily selected as being "pure" or "typical." Goethe knew no such abstraction, and it can have no pertinence to his work; his own sketches of various phases of the Renaissance and its types, from which I quote extensively, are quite a different matter.

An impediment to understanding may possibly arise from the very nature of this study, in that a valid judgment of its parts can in some instances be made only against the background of the whole. If the reader should choose to take issue with each point as it comes up, many a statement, assumption, or conclusion in the early chapters may at first seem unfounded or inappropriate, especially if judged according to the conventional approaches to *Faust*. Some sections may not receive their full treatment and demonstration till later, for the evidence is cumulative. The material is so manifold and complexly interconnected that the full pattern of relationship can only gradually come to view.

Even in the matter of preliminary fundamentals there are wide possibilities for misunderstanding. For instance, the fact that many new sources and analogues are brought forward, does not mean that my main purpose is the study of unknown influences on the work. Nor does the establishment of the Renaissance background of thought and symbol in *Faust* mean that I think of it as a historical drama with a sixteenth-century setting. Altogether, it seemed advisable in the first chapter and later, to take more than ordinary precautions about establishing basic principles and points of departure.

The chronological period understood by my use of the term Renaissance is naturally not limited to the generation of the historical Faust, but extends from the age of Nicolaus Cusanus of mid-fifteenth century to the early seventeenth century, a period which for the purposes of this study constitutes an unbroken continuum, with all its successive mutations in vital sensitiveness, through early Baroque. It is more amusing than alarming to see the Baroque shoved farther and farther back into the sixteenth century—and often for reasons that can be found equally well in the fifteenth century! We may indeed soon expect to see Baroque and Gothic shaking hands across the body of a shrunken and expired Renaissance. Of course, a fuller insight into the true nature of late Renaissance mannerism and its intrinsic difference from the Baroque (despite superficial similarities to it) would have prevented the current confusions—but that is really a minor matter of terminologies. Goethe himself, as we shall see, considered the fifteenth and sixteenth centuries as a historical unit and a great age of mankind.

Beyond its specific purpose, this new approach and perspective may be useful in contributing toward an increasing objectification of attitude toward *Faust*. We can proceed to find out what the poem means, without first having to worry about what it means to us. We can cast off the unnecessary personal burden of imagining either that we ourselves are latter-day Fausts or that we must take issue with the characters, events, and conclusions of the drama, seeing them in terms of our own ideals and passing personal or contemporary judgments upon them. If we can cease to take our own attitudes toward *Faust* so seriously, that alone will go far toward clarifying many a murky problem. It will also be a relief not to feel obliged to take seriously as *Faust* criticism the interpretations from subjective or "modern" points of view. They have their place, to be sure, as symptoms or revelations of our times, but the work they are talking about is not really the *Faust* that Goethe planned and wrote. There is a complacent saying that every man has his own *Hamlet*, or his own *Faust*, but there are very few who have any reason to be proud of their personal constructions and none at all who have achieved the fullness and profundity of Shakespeare's *Hamlet* or of Goethe's *Faust*. On the other hand, any further extension of our view of the real dimensions, or the true limits, of the work is to be commended and taken seriously.

If, finally, we can learn to read *Faust* like one of its older peers, like the *Aeneid*, the *Divine Comedy, Don Quixote*, or even like the *Hamlet* we have learned to know in the last few decades, that is, to read it with all warmth, delight, and personal participation but without any subjective involvement, without any urge to accept or reject, if we can regard it as an artistic phenomenon which, like a natural phenomenon, simply is there, as it is, and has to be taken as it is—when we reach that level, then we have come to full maturity in our reading of this masterpiece also. It will stand before us fresh and bright in its own clear colors, with its own full, deep resonance. Once we have learned to understand the poem by itself and against its full background, then we shall be more truly able to estimate what it means to us and to our times.

Needless to say, this study by its very nature cannot hope to attain to such a level of ultimate objectivity, but its aim is in that direction. Establishing the Renaissance background of Goethe's dramatic poem is an important preliminary step away from the two kinds of subjectivity and toward a fuller understanding of it on its own terms. Exploring its areas of relationship to antiquity is a task of which much still remains to be done, surprisingly enough; at various places, especially in chapters six and seven, I have called attention to neglected areas of classical influence which are important for the understanding of the work though I could do so only briefly and incidentally. However, as many examples will illustrate, ancient thought and literature often came into the work through the medium of the Renaissance.

This is not at all a complete study of the subject from the stated point of view. Only a select part of the material I have at hand has been utilized and only a limited number of phases and sequences in *Faust*, generally the more problematic ones, have been re-examined. The reader should, therefore, not be surprised if I fail even to mention a number of obviously Renaissance passages, if I take up only a few motifs of the Gretchen tragedy, and if I am concerned with the second part only in so far as there are connecting lines from the first part that have not previously been observed. I have, as a rule, excluded any specific detail of Renaissance influence, however interesting in itself, if it did not contribute to larger phases of the understanding and interpretation of the work as a whole.

Since the quotations used are from six languages, I deemed it best to give them all in English in the body of the text, and to relegate the foreign originals to the notes (except for a few words or brief phrases). For general readability, as well as consistency, it seemed desirable to give also the *Faust* passages in English translation, usually in the George Madison Priest version, except where even greater faithfulness to the original was necessary, as in the final "Chorus mysticus." The other passages from Goethe's works are generally in my own translation; where previous translations exist, I have consulted them and have gratefully taken over from them various felicitous phrases and even whole sentences, though they could hardly ever have been used unrevised.

The notes are fuller and more elaborate than I should normally make them, and that for a good reason. Any such new interpretation as this, if it is to hope for acceptance, has the obligation to prove its validity at every step of the way. No reader, no scholar of *Faust* could be expected to depart from a century and more of critical consensus unless the reasons for departing were clear and convincing and were presented in such a way that he could check the evidence for himself at every point. Though a scholarly "apparatus" does not have within itself any powers of self-justification, special circumstances can not only justify it, but demand it.

When the new insights set forth in this study first dawned on me, some eight years ago, my first reaction was one of surprise and doubt. Even after more and more convincing evidence gradually accumulated, an attitude of cautious reserve persisted. When the manuscript of this study was finished, I therefore asked several of our most eminent Goethe scholars whether they would be willing to subject it to a severe critical scrutiny; they kindly consented to do so, and only after they had read it, and after a large group of Germanists at the meeting of the Modern Language Association in 1949 had reacted favorably toward a paper on the theme, did I venture to submit it for publication. Since then several other qualified scholars have read the manuscript, and I am most grateful to all for their valuable criticisms and suggestions. Their kind encouragement reassured me; their dissent in certain matters of interpretation and point of view was in every case given serious consideration and in many cases led to a modification of my statement or to a fuller and clearer exposition.

In fact, a great deal of time this past year was spent in rewriting the manuscript from beginning to end; whole sections and one whole chapter are almost entirely new, and on several important points where doubts had been expressed I now include the full background of evidence. Ultimately, of course, I have had to make up my own mind on every point, even as I have to and wish to assume full responsibility for all I maintain, without implying in advance that my kind and able critics have committed themselves to that point of view. The very newness of the field will almost inevitably bring with it errors and oversights. Even though I have exer-

cised all due caution, it is within the nature of human fallibility that some errors will have remained. Even as I hope that my new findings and interpretations will be received with an open mind, I also hope I shall always keep my mind open to better and fuller evidence and gladly abandon any position which proves to be untenable.

The register of my indebtedness is a large one. I am most grateful to those colleagues of mine who gave of their own precious time to read this manuscript and to make suggestions for its improvement: to Professors Lawrence M. Price of the University of California, Carl F. Schreiber of Yale University, Meno Spann of Northwestern University, Heinrich Meyer of Muhlenberg College, Heinrich Henel of the University of Wisconsin, and William S. Heckscher of the University of Iowa. The last named I single out for special thanks, since he so generously put at my disposal one of his own discoveries and also, as an art historian, has cast his expert eye upon my exposition of those unrecognized phases of Goethe's poetic symbolism which have their origins in Renaissance art. These phases could only be treated summarily within the scope of this book; a separate, more detailed study of them is completed and will, I hope, appear soon. My deepest gratitude also goes to a very perceptive reader here at home who has always courageously consented to be the first representative of the intelligent general reader and thus to smooth the way for those who may follow.

A glance through the notes will indicate how great is my debt to the work of earlier Goethe scholars. I did have to take issue with them in certain matters and often could not fittingly indicate my profound regard for them in other matters; I therefore take this opportunity to do so. Far from rejecting past scholarship (as I may seem to do in many a passage), I am clearly aware that I am rather continuing it in the present, and concurring with its results in many important respects. It will be noticed that my debt to scholars in other fields is perhaps even greater, principally to those intellectual historians and those art historians who have brought the symbolic world of the Renaissance, in all its attractiveness, to life again for our age. Without their once mentioning the great poem in the contexts that were most valuable to me, they did bring to new and fuller life for me that ultimate and glorious statement of the symbolic understanding of life which is Goethe's *Faust*.

My greatest intellectual and spiritual indebtedness I reserve for special mention in conclusion. It is to the dean of American Goethe scholars, Alexander Rudolf Hohlfeld. His active interest in this study and his cogent criticisms and constructive suggestions are reflected in many important revisions. After seventeen years it was a pleasure to find myself his pupil once again. His advice was the most valuable I received. No student ever had more just cause to revere a great teacher, and I dedicate this work to him, with the sincere hope that he may find it worthy of his exacting standards and noble example.

HAROLD JANTZ

Northwestern University
Evanston, Illinois
August, 1950

CONTENTS

Goethe's Faust

AS A RENAISSANCE MAN

CHAPTER I

THE BACKGROUND

N THE CRITICAL STUDY of Goethe's *Faust* during the past century it seems to have become traditional to regard this great work as essentially a subjective expression of the ideas and tendencies of the poet and his age, and to interpret it on this basis in all but a few details and externalities. The validity of this point of view I should not wish to call into question, but its exclusiveness or even primacy as a guiding principle in interpretation I do see weighty reasons for re-examining. There is a large body of evidence, much of it hitherto overlooked, which points to the conclusion that Goethe from the very beginning intended to present Faust objectively as a man of the Renaissance whose thoughts and actions are in just correspondence to the intellectual and spiritual climate of those times.[1]

This does not in the least imply that Goethe was here creating character and action which were alien to his own personal attitudes and convictions. It implies just the opposite, if we may anticipate, namely, that he must have felt a natural attraction to the Renaissance, a natural predisposition toward its ways of thinking and feeling. Otherwise he could hardly have brought his masterpiece into such intrinsic harmony with a period not his own. We can indeed think of him as not being limited to the prevailing attitudes, and as seeking in the past for what he could not find fully, richly, truly in his own age. This goes much deeper than the revolt of the other young men of his "Storm and Stress" generation, who also went back to a more glamorous age of the past and tried their hand at the Faust and other Renaissance themes.

We all know how much Goethe found that was cognate

to his deepest self in Graeco-Roman antiquity, how greatly this enriched his life, and helped him to enrich our lives. On the other hand, there has been hardly any searching examination of his sympathetic relationship to the Renaissance even though there was much in him which came to fullest expression in his harmonious response to those times.

What is generally designated as "influence" may, for the truly creative artist, be no more than a discovery of affinity; he generally has a natural inclination toward that which he borrows. But this does not make influence unimportant, because this very act of discovery often brings about a development of the weak, vague, subjective urges and impulses within the artist into strong, clear, objective conviction and expression in the work of art. For example, it is quite possible that Goethe could have written a kind of *Faust* subjectively and from his own times, with no Renaissance mirroring and only slight local coloring, but such a work could never have had the magnificent scope, the perennial validity, the symbolic depth and coherence which his true *Faust* attained in the act of creative objectification. The more subjective and "modern" Fausts of other authors around and after Goethe demonstrate this all too painfully.

The seeking for and finding of congenial influences first makes possible the full productive realization of an inner impulse. This, as we shall see, Goethe himself observed and emphasized. Thus there is no need to deny the validity of the standard interpretations. *Faust* is indeed expressive of its author personally and also of some secondary tendencies of the eighteenth century. This old thesis is certainly true, but just as certainly incomplete and inadequate. The old and the new are not mutually contradictory, but complementary. Goethe found himself and his Faust in the Renaissance.

From this it is, no doubt, already clear that when I speak of the Renaissance elements in *Faust*, I mean something far beyond mere verbal echoes or thematic parallels. Indeed, the chief concern of this study will be to show that the larger complexes within the drama, and actually the overall patterns, are distinctly Renaissance in character rather than eighteenth century from the period of Goethe's youth and after. My first awareness of this came indirectly in the course of studies on the Renaissance background of seventeenth-century Anglo-German and American-German relations. It came most specifically as a result of my study of John Winthrop the Younger (1606-1676), the most "Faustian" of early Americans, and of his circle of friends in Europe, their projects and enterprises, and particularly of his remarkable library (so heavily German in content) which led me to the heart of the matter.[2]

Incidentally, several of the books in Winthrop's library which are most relevant to this study had previously belonged to a Renaissance Englishman, who in his life anticipated so much of Faust as Goethe envisioned him. I refer to John Dee (1527-1608), one of the most honored scholars of his day, who had traversed all the charted fields of knowledge, had come to the same bitter conclusion as to their futility, and turned from them to magic, as he records in a memorable passage in his journal, to inquire from the spirits he summons about those inner and ultimate truths he had sought for in vain. In quite a different way John Dee also was mocked and rejected by these spirits, though popular opinion all through his life credited him with high success in occult matters. With his sinister companion, Edward Kelley, evil and indispensable, he set out for the court of the Emperor Rudolph II at Prague. Except for his fleeting success with the Emperor, the parallel ceases here, and Dee returned to England a deeply frustrated and disappointed man.[3] There is, however, one last parallel: he had like old Faust the grand vision of new land and a new commonwealth, specifically in America, though we have only the titles of his lost manuscripts on the subject, together with a few other incidental references, to tell us how his vision took shape.[4]

How very much closer even this first parallel is to Goethe's Faust than is either the historical or the legendary Faust of the sixteenth century! Indeed, it would seem that one of the chief barriers to the understanding of the Goethean character and his Renaissance background has been the excessive accompanying concern with the historical and legendary Fausts, who stem from a very different cultural environment in that period. Fascinating as they are in themselves, they contributed little to Goethe's concept, aside from the names and the superficial suggestions of a few incidents and motifs. Even some of the "analogies" which are regularly pointed out are rather far-fetched. As a result of this habit of referring to the folk book, Marlowe's drama, and the puppet play (and alas, the opera), there are still to this day many persons who believe that the Faust in Goethe's drama summons up the devil, makes an old-fashioned pact with him, and either is hauled off to Hell or escapes by some sophism.

It was not only Faust who was taken over merely in name. Mephistopheles, too, and Wagner are entirely different in character and function from their namesakes in the Faust book. I emphasize these commonplaces because it is here that the crucial misunderstanding, as I see it, has occurred. As a result of the entirely new content that Goethe created for these mere husks of name and incident, it has been assumed generally that the new spirit, the utterly different line of development can only be explained as subjectively Goethean, as Storm and Stress in origin. Thus the Renaissance parallels and references which do admittedly occur are usually dismissed as mere bits of local color without organic function or significance.[5] There is, of course, some truth to this claim of personal, subjective origin; Goethe did recast the materials in the mold of his own soul, according to his own innermost feelings and perceptions. But it does not follow that this recasting made his version substantially anachronistic; on the contrary, whatever in the drama expresses his personal principles and ideals does so because these happened to be in accord with the spirit of the Renaissance. Typically eighteenth-century convictions of his which would not fit into this setting he expressed in such contemporary works as *Wilhelm Meister*.

The false inference of subjectivity and anachronism was unfortunately furthered by the general run of background reading in the Renaissance which has accompanied the study of *Faust*. Such reading was concentrated too exclusively on books in witchcraft and demonology; these may account for scme peripheral details in the drama, but they do not account for anything of intrinsic importance. Even in this occult field the more sophisticated and boldly unorthodox books have been largely neglected although one of the most characteristic features of Goethe's work is the subtle, knowledgeable, and highly symbolical manner in which he introduces occult concepts and phenomena. And it is not until we have gone beyond this field entirely that we come upon the fundamental Renaissance affinities to the work.

Many a scholar has, of course, called attention to Renaissance and other older sources for one or the other detail in the drama; but only two scholars, apparently, have written considerable studies which specifically attribute the fundamental Goethean transformation of *Faust* to influences from the past. Julius Goebel proposed the ancient Neoplatonist, Iamblichus, as the chief source; Agnes Bartscherer proposed Paracelsus, though both of them also gave other references from antiquity and the Renaissance for various specific details.[6] There is a strictly limited though important truth to the claims of both; what caused them to claim too much for their new discoveries was that they had not ranged far enough in classical and Renaissance thought and literature to view their findings in the proper perspective. Goethe, as will be seen, was affected not so much by ancient Neoplatonism as by the Renaissance transformation of it which gave it a new dynamism, a new relation to the activistic age of science and discovery.[7]

As for Paracelsus, the character of Faust and the total configuration of the drama have in their larger aspects less to do with the personality and destiny of this revolutionary philosopher than they have with those of several other Renaissance men. It is nevertheless true that much of the thought in *Faust* is Neoplatonic and Paracelsian, and also that there are a number of separate new insights in Goebel, and especially in Bartscherer, which we cannot afford to neglect even though we are unable to accept their main theses or many of their specific claims. As we shall see, there is no one paramount source for *Faust*.

Incidentally, the important revival of Stoicism in the Renaissance as it affected Goethe seems not to have received the attention it deserves, perhaps for this reason: whereas the ethical writings of the late Stoa have remained well known, there has been a general neglect of the natural philosophy of the middle Stoa, and it is precisely this which deeply impressed him from youth onward. The intellectual position maintained is remarkably germane to Goethe's, with its pantheistic monism subsuming in unity the whole range of the material and spiritual in an unbroken series of metamorphoses, the subordination of evil to the Divine purpose active in the world, the affirmation of the truth of phenomena and the reliability of the senses when guided by reason and experience. For this philosophy man and light occupy a central position in the single continuum of the corporeal and spiritual, of matter and force. But this study is hardly the place to take up these largely neglected relations. Suffice it to say that Goethe had easy access to the Stoic cosmology by way of its popular transmitters, especially Cicero, whom he read throughout his life with far more interest and affection than he did the Neoplatonists. We shall have occasion in later chapters to observe a few significant illustrations of his inclination toward Stoic and Neo-Pythagorean concepts.

Certain basic assumptions traditional in Goethe scholarship may cause initial resistance to the idea that the young poet intended to present as objectively as possible a man whose attitudes, problems, and actions are conditioned by the Renaissance. We have always been told, and recently as emphatically as ever, that Goethe, especially as a young man, was an "Erlebnisdichter" who created primarily out of his own personal experience, and that every significant work of his was autobiographical in its inception, a fragment of a great confession. This assertion is obviously true but we may have to modify our ideas as to its scope and meaning when we observe other characteristics of his creative activity and when we add certain statements of his which are also true and quite undeniable.

First and clearest of all is the phenomenon of *Götz von Berlichingen*. This drama, like *Faust*, has its setting in the early sixteenth century. The author's initial creative impulse for both works came at about the same time, in late 1769 and early 1770, as he tells us. The actual writing on both probably did not begin until a few years later. *Götz* was quickly finished but *Faust* was not. Now *Götz* is a centrally significant work of Goethe's; the specifically autobiographical material in it is relatively small and not at all primary though we may be sure that he put his whole soul into the drama and imaginatively lived through and experienced its whole course of events. Intrinsically the drama is an amazingly clear-sighted and historically valid presentation of the upset of a traditional social equilibrium by the intrusion of new factors, when Roman law and Renaissance court life came into ascendancy around a new type of territorial tyrant. The result was tragedy for those who persisted in the old customs, laws, and principles, and also for those who followed the new trends against their deeper convictions and loyalties. Two statements from the conversations with Eckermann will give Goethe's own views on the matter, the second being necessary for the correct understanding of the first. The first reads: "I wrote my *Götz von Berlichingen* as a young man of twenty-two, and was astonished ten years later at the truth of my representation. I had, of course, not experienced or seen anything of the kind and therefore must have possessed the knowledge of manifold human circumstances by anticipation."[8] The clear implication here is that the autobiographical "confessional" factor was not of any importance.

That Goethe did not have the full personal experience of what went into *Götz* by the age of twenty-two, we can readily grant, as we can also grant his notion of anticipation in the restricted form it developed later in the conversation, in connection with *Faust*. There he applied it only to the intuitive poetic insight into fundamental human reactions, distinguishing these from the phenomena that have to be observed before they can be reported truly. But unless we are willing to succumb to occult psychology, we must assume that he had by the age of twenty-two assimilated the knowledge and background that went into his *Götz*, not in actual experience of course, but vicariously through his historical-legal studies and his voluminous reading. The intuitive part was the uncanny sureness with which his understanding went to the historical heart of the matter, so that when the time of creation came, he could start from a true outline and a firm foundation.

Goethe himself implied this in answer to Eckermann's next remark that there was not a line in the whole of *Faust* that did not bear the traces of a careful study of the world and of life: "That may be so; however, if I had not already carried the world in myself by anticipation, I would have remained blind with seeing eyes and all my research and experience would have been nothing but a completely dead and futile effort. The light is there and the colors surround us, but if we carried no light and no colors in our own eye, we would also not perceive any such thing outside ourselves."[9] Thus to him "Erlebnisdichtung" clearly meant an inner correspondence to outer phenomena, a variant of the old idea of the correspondence of the microcosm to the macrocosm. A bit later we shall hear him state this even more plainly.

With this as his meaning, it amounts virtually to the same thing whether we call his reshaping of the *Faust* subjective or objective (he himself referred to it in both ways). His subjectivity was not of the willful and arbitrary kind which destroyed the inner harmony and historical veracity of the work; it was, instead, of the conserving, reverent kind which raised the work to a higher level within its own (and his own) sphere. The reciprocity between subject and object young Goethe brought out with especial clearness in his letter of August 21, 1774, to Fritz Jacobi in connection with the reworking of a section of Beaumarchais' memoirs into his *Clavigo*. In a different way he did the same with reference to Rembrandt in the last paragraph of "Nach Falkonet und über Falkonet."[10]

On various occasions during his life he took care to point out how conscientiously he strove for historical truthfulness in the three great Renaissance dramas of his youth, *Götz*, *Faust*, and *Egmont*. In his autobiography, in connection with his visits to Darmstadt in the spring of 1772, he said: "*Faust* was already under way, *Götz von Berlichingen* was gradually being built up in my mind, the study of the fifteenth and sixteenth centuries engrossed me. . . ."[11] In the fourth section of his annals, in telling about his abandoned project for writing the life of the colorful seventeenth-century hero, Duke Bernhard of Weimar, he concluded: "For me this effort was not without fruit . . . just as the studies for *Götz* and *Egmont* afforded me deeper insights into the fifteenth and sixteenth centuries. . . ."[12] Finally in a conversation of 1825 he stated:

"I wrote *Egmont* in the year 1775, that is, fifty years ago. I remained very faithful to history and strove for the utmost veracity."[13] By this he naturally meant veracity of historic essentials, as he made clear in his subsequent remarks on his change of the hero to a young man.

Surely it must be of significance in his creative life that among the dramas which he was able to complete, *Götz*, *Egmont, Faust*, and *Tasso* all have their setting in the Renaissance; only one, *Iphigenie*, is set in antiquity; only *Clavigo*, *Stella*, and several even less significant plays have a contemporary setting—all the rest which are of any importance were abandoned as fragments lacking the necessary inner vitality and urgency to bring them to a successful conclusion. He carried through a contemporary theme and plot with high distinction only in narrative form, prose or verse.

Goethe made his clearest statement on poetic objectivity in 1826: "As long as the poet merely expresses his own few subjective perceptions, he cannot yet be called a poet; but as soon as he knows how to make the world his own and to express it, he is a poet. And then he is inexhaustible and can be always new, whereas a subjective nature has soon expressed the little which is inside it and at last perishes in mannerism." And almost immediately thereafter in the same conversation: "Every worthy effort, on the contrary, turns from within to the world, as you can see in all great epochs which were really engaged in striving and progressing and were all of an objective nature." This, as Eckermann remarks, turned the conversation "especially to the great age of the fifteenth and sixteenth centuries."[14]

An earlier statement of Goethe's may help to explain why *Faust* was misinterpreted from the very first, by some of the author's closest associates, and especially by the Romantics: "My whole period was different from me, for it was completely engrossed in a subjective direction, whereas I in my objective efforts stood quite alone and at a disadvantage."[15]

That young Goethe lived up to old Goethe's specifications can be clearly seen from a letter which Gottlob Friedrich Ernst, Freiherr von Schönborn wrote to Heinrich Wilhelm von Gerstenberg, October 11, 1773: "He indeed possesses, so far as I know him, an exceptionally discerning poetic gift which is capable of feeling its way into objects through and through, so that everything becomes specific and individual in his mind."[16]

Goethe's whole creative life illustrates his will toward objectification. Whatever his personal involvement at its inception, the literary work quickly developed beyond the function of mere self-expression, rising to the level of a clear-sighted, dispassionate portrayal, often still higher to the level of symbolic representation, so that in the end the initial personal factors faded into insignificance. Along with these extraordinary powers of creation and objectification there was his insight into history and its motive forces. His intuitive understanding of certain intrinsic aspects of the Renaissance was not matched again (with various partial exceptions) for the next hundred years.

And yet, how was it possible for Goethe to have filled his characters and their actions with the true living spirit of those times? And why was it that nineteenth-century and subsequent scholars perceived not the essentially but only the incidentally Renaissance nature of his work? A part of the answer, beyond what has already been suggested, may be that his youth fell in a time when the full natural Renaissance tradition (though modified in late, in last Baroque) was still alive and continuous in certain circles, not yet blighted and dessicated by Rationalism, and not yet swamped by the new material of changing times, whereas the nineteenth-century historians, coming after the decisive break in the tradition, gave the world an incomplete picture of the period, from which the figure of the Goethean Faust could not be understood.[17]

Thus it escaped general attention that many of the Faustian phenomena which were considered to have their sources in the eighteenth century could be found much more vividly and fully exemplified in the sixteenth century. The hypothesis of Swedenborg's influence, for example, is still accepted on faith in some commentaries though an impressive series of eminent scholars has shown it to be dubious, or even illusory, and although the few lines which it seems to account for can be better illustrated and explained from other sources.[18]

Actually, Goethe himself as a mature man felt that sharp break with the Renaissance-Baroque tradition, as we can see so plainly when in the 1780's and 1790's he took up the *Faust* again to try to bring it to completion. His and Schiller's remarks about finding the lost thread again are significant. Also symptomatic are the derogatory epithets he kept hurling at the onerous fragment which continued to haunt him and would not be banished. Only as he entered old age did he make his peace again with his creation, and with real sympathy, often covered over with a self-protecting layer of humor, did he further its unfolding life. But even in his period of outward aversion his sure poetic intuition had not allowed the work to be diverted from its destined course, and he later remained conscious of having resisted Schiller's deflecting influences.[19]

During the last few decades fresh insights into several vital aspects of the Renaissance have opened up new ways to the understanding of Goethe's poetic intent. Out of the Warburg Institute, to give just one example, came that distinguished group of art historians, and others such as the philosopher Ernst Cassirer, who again read Renaissance books which had gone virtually unread, or had been misread, for a hundred and fifty years and more. These books had been ejected from the accepted canon of what the eighteenth century considered reasonable and what the nineteenth century thought the Renaissance ought to have been. The interpretation of art in the vital areas where its cultural and symbolic aspects coincide with those of literature is of primary importance for the literary historian also. For instance, Panofsky and Saxl's elucidation of Dürer's engraving "Melencolia I," on the basis of an exact and detailed knowledge of Renaissance symbolic connotations, sheds not a little light on the first scene of the *Urfaust*.[20] The hundreds of volumes still preserved in the Winthrop library served me as an introduction to many phases of Renaissance thinking and speculation, and it was in my search for light on these trains of thought, slighted in the older scholarly works, that I came to the modern studies of the group just mentioned as well as of Will-Erich Peuckert and others.

The library of Goethe's father and the many other libraries to which Goethe had access in his youth contained a large number of books which could have initiated the young man into those fast-disappearing ways of thinking. There were, for instance, the art books and the polyhistorical reference works belonging to father Goethe, the art books being particularly important for introducing the youth to those symbolic borderline fields of iconography for which later generations lost understanding. One recondite and fascinating complex of Renaissance thought was added in the books to which he was introduced by Susanna von Klettenberg and Dr. Metz during his critical illness and convalescence at Frankfurt. His fondness for old and out-of-the-way books of the fifteenth to seventeenth century continued through the whole period of the actual writing of the *Urfaust*, and beyond that, as we can gather from direct and indirect allusions of his.[21]

His caustic remarks on several occasions indicate that Goethe's turning for comfort and inspiration to a past century was largely due to his acute feeling of antipathy for his own century because of its aridity and artificiality.[22] His genius, however, was broad enough to recognize the good qualities of his age and to deal with them fairly in other works where they were pertinent. True, his aversion is in large measure part of the general revolt of his Storm and Stress generation against the literary standards, the social and intellectual norms of the eighteenth century. Several other members of Goethe's age group were attracted, in passing, to the Renaissance and even attempted Fausts of their own. However, such a superficial attraction to the uninhibited vitality and marvelous recklessness of the period, without any sense of its intrinsic character, cannot be compared with Goethe's deep apperception. Only two achieved anything like an artistic feeling for that era: Wilhelm Heinse in his sensuous evocation of the art and pleasure of the sixteenth century, and Johann Gottfried Herder in his critical-literary studies which brought so much of the German and general European past to life for his age. Herder did not favor the Renaissance, except in the case of Shakespeare, until after his meeting with Goethe at Strassburg, and it may well be that his subsequent broader interest in the period was stimulated by Goethe. Yet the Renaissance was probably at no time preeminent or artistically determining for Herder; and even for Heinse only one artistic and social complex of it really came to life. Neither of them shows any marked concern for the Renaissance approach to ultimates in human life and destiny which so absorbed and fascinated Goethe. The older poet, Wieland, on the other hand, here and there displays a remarkably keen understanding of the period, and we know that he was a sympathetic sharer of Goethe's interest during their early years together at Weimar.

In Goethe alone, then, do we find (despite certain lapses and misconceptions) a profound knowledge of the secret springs and moving forces of the Renaissance, a knowledge of such scope and truth that every advancement of our understanding of the period seems to make his artistic grasp of it appear in an ever more favorable light. This, however, especially in the case of *Faust*, is what still remains to be demonstrated.

The present study is chiefly concerned with the *Faust* of Goethe's youth, or at any rate takes this *Urfaust* as its point of departure, because a sharper focus on the main problems is made possible thereby and because the sources and proto-types of the early parts are not as well known as those of parts written later. The chief reason, however, is that a study of the Renaissance background of the *Urfaust* reveals inti-mate connections in intent and purpose to the completed drama which have not been previously observed. Thus the unity of the work from its original inception finds further confirmation, and Goethe's own precepts for the interpreta-tion of the third act, the Helena drama, will be found to ap-ply to the whole: "The main intention is clear and the whole plain; the details likewise will be and become that if we do not try to examine and explain the parts by themselves, but rather elucidate them in relation to the whole."[23]

In the matter of general background, it is the sections of *Faust* written before November, 1775, when Goethe came to Weimar, that lie in deepest obscurity. He mentioned only a few suggestive sources then and later, not by any means all of them or even the main ones. In the middle period of the agonizingly slow completion of the first part we have more ample references to the variety of old books which he read in a resolute and sometimes futile attempt to put himself back into the Faustian world. But even for this period and for later there is evidence that other unmentioned books may have been fully as influential, if not more so.

It is important that there be no misunderstanding on one point: the Renaissance parallels and prototypes brought for-ward in this study are not necessarily to be considered as direct sources for *Faust*. In some instances it would have been possible to give numerous other parallels and prototypes from that period, most of which would be closer to the work than any from the eighteenth century. Since similar thought and action sequences are to be found in many books of the period, there is often no way of knowing exactly which books provided the chief imaginative stimuli for Goethe. On the other hand, it is true that a few of the possible sources are particularly close to his concepts or have a larger pattern of correspondence to his drama; they may stand, provisionally at least, as sources. In a few cases also, where Goethe himself suggested the source and his suggestion has not been followed up, we now have definite confirmation. Before turning to the main character, let us first establish a broader background of relations to the Renaissance by a closer examination of Wagner, Mephistopheles, and the aerial spirits.

CHAPTER II

THREE PRELIMINARY EXAMPLES:
WAGNER, MEPHISTOPHELES, AND THE
AERIAL SPIRITS

F WE WISH TO BEGIN with an especially clear exemplification of Goethe's Renaissance design, from the *Urfaust* onward, we can find it in the figure of Wagner. Seen generally, he is the pedant of any period, a likeable pedant it is true, without guile or envy, and with the further mitigating trait of an appreciation for genius which has caused him to hitch his little wagon load of learning to Faust's star. Seen closely, however, the very exact details given as to his attitudes and aims can apply in their totality only to the typical humanist of the fifteenth to seventeenth century, and not to the scholar of a later period.

Wagner's first speech (on declaiming a Greek tragedy) and those that follow show his complete devotion to the rhetorical tradition, the formalism and verbal elegance, the concentration upon the technique of delivery and the art of persuasion, which was the ideal of the pure humanist as we find it both in the text books of the day and in the most highly praised of authors. For example, as Cassirer has pointed out, the earlier fifteenth-century humanists (with the exception of Cusanus) based their preference for Plato over Aristotle almost exclusively on the divine eloquence of the one as contrasted with the prosaic dryness of the other; and their study of Plato was almost entirely philological rather than philosophical.[1] Since Cicero was for them the exalted model of verbal elegance (rather than the philosophical or political thinker), Ciceronianism is the characterizing epithet applied to this attitude; and the singular emptiness, or at best derivativeness of content, is what has since been most often noted about many a highly polished humanist who overawed his contemporaries.

Even at that time, however, there was sharp criticism, and the formalist incurred the scorn of the integralist for whom eloquence was not an external technique but an inner gift, a special function of true knowledge and conviction, arising spontaneously out of insight and permitting its communication. Wagner's lament about the difficulty of learning the art of persuasion in the seclusion of his study is countered by Faust's statement:

> "Unless you feel, you never will attain it;
> Unless this feeling pours forth from your soul
> With native, pleasing vigor to control
> The hearts of all your hearers, it will be in vain."

This assertion of the indissoluble union of form and content is re-echoed even verbally in the first little critical essay in "From Goethe's Notebook" of 1775, with a metaphor added from Renaissance alchemy: "Every form, even the most deeply felt, has something untrue about it; yet it is, after all, the glass through which we gather the divine rays of far-flung nature to a fiery focus on the hearts of men. But the glass! To whom it is not given, he will not attain it; it is, like the mysterious stone of the alchemists, vessel and material, fire and balneum."[2]

Wagner's pompous modesty, used for purely decorative purposes, his sententious clichés, his use of such expressions as "Museum" for study, "kritisches Bestreben," and "Quellen" (even his formalistic "modernism"), together with Faust's derogatory remarks, show clearly that Goethe envisioned him as the typical scholar of the Renaissance for whom the sacred source was an old manuscript and the chief end of learning was to issue a critical edition of some Greek or Roman work in which he could annotate every word with every shred of pertinent and impertinent learning at his command. For such a "trash barrel" and "rummage room" ("Ein Kehrichtfass und eine Rumpelkammer") one can turn to many a learned and bulky tome of the period with its mass of erudition, more of it learned display than genuine elucidation. Naturally, true scholars and real works of scholarship originated alongside these while, on the other hand, the penchant of pedants for indiscriminate fullness did not die out with the Renaissance though it was most prevalent at that time.

The motif of the manuscript, the parchment, turns up again toward the end of the Easter Walk where Wagner envisions his highest bliss in the life of a humanist antiquarian, and is told by Faust that he is aware of only one drive. His one drive here referred to, his antiquarianism, specifically the obsession for old manuscripts, was a decidedly strong one throughout that period. It is most dramatically illustrated in the far-flung travels of Poggio to Swiss, German, French, and English monasteries in search of manuscripts of the ancient writers and perhaps most typically seen in the correspondence of the humanists ("ex museo meo"), whose chilly elegance always comes to a glow at the mention of a "codex vetustissimus" of any ancient author, even of one on veterinary medicine. Quite different from this antiquarian drive, which produced a long line of happy humanists of high and low esteem, was the other drive which Faust adjures Wagner never to learn to know. That was the drive with which many of the Renaissance geniuses of passionate energy were imbued and which tore their souls between the strong earthly lust for life and the powerful transcendent seeking after ultimates in philosophy and art—but more of that in its proper place.

Wagner is evidently intended by Goethe to be a graphic Renaissance counterpart to Faust. If I were to name one actual humanist with Wagner's characteristics, Claudius Salmasius comes dangerously close in many respects, in view of his enormous miscellaneous knowledge and his imposing lack of judgment. Also his predecessor at Leyden, Joseph Scaliger, the son of Julius Caesar Scaliger, was in many ways an engaging prototype and shuffled around rather forlornly in his father's over-large shoes. But there were dozens of other Wagners busily adding their bit toward the "revival of learning."[3]

It would be an error to consider Goethe's attitude toward the typical humanist as completely satirical and hostile. Here, as always, the poet's magnificent objectivity asserts itself: he exposes Wagner's weaknesses and pretensions, but he does so with affectionate humor and real warmth so that in the end we have an indulgent liking for the harmless, happy academician.

If Goethe had conceived of Wagner as a typical eighteenth-century pedant, he could not have made him change over from the humanist rhetorician and antiquarian of the first part to the alchemical experimenter of the second part without violating every law of consistency and probability. The career of an eighteenth-century scholar simply did not take such a course. On the other hand, the career of a sixteenth-century scholar could and frequently did take such a course. We need only think of the life of Michael Toxites. In his youth he was an esteemed Neo-Latin poet and he wrote commentaries on Cicero's orations which were used far into the following century. Later in life he became one of the three foremost Paracelsians, devoting himself thenceforward to alchemy and alchemical medicine, to the editing of Paracelsian and pseudo-Paracelsian writings.[4]

This is only the first of numerous instances where we shall be able to see clearly that an interpretation in eighteenth-century terms involves the drama as a whole in discrepancies and inconsistencies, whereas an interpretation in Renaissance terms makes these seeming discrepancies vanish and allows the natural coherence and consistency of the poet's intent to be manifest.

Goethe's Mephistopheles also has little intrinsic connection with his namesake of the Faust book, but his relations to the Renaissance are many and varied. To the best of my knowledge no one has yet fully traced the literary ancestry of this paradoxical, ironical negativist, this jester who cannot refrain even from making fun of himself and of his function in the scheme of things. We shall not survey the long list of disabused, hardbitten, clever, amoral Renaissance prototypes, the kind of men who, convinced of the inherent baseness of man, prided themselves on not being taken in by any higher ideals or values. They delighted in exposing these as mere masks behind which the true, base motives of mankind lurked, and in acting and advising to action in a cynically depraved manner as a token of their honesty and lack of sham. One lurid sink of corruption and evil calculation was Pietro Aretino. Another Renaissance man who traditionally exemplifies the brutal frankness of founding the principles of political action upon an unmoral calculation of human baseness and weakness is Niccolò Machiavelli. The adjectives Machiavellian and Mephistophelean have overlapping areas of meaning in the European languages.

However, there is a better and closer prototype for Mephistopheles, not only in himself, but in his intimate association with the "Faustian" in the Renaissance. And this larger context is naturally much more significant than any piecemeal parallels. I refer to the figure of Luigi Pulci (1432-1484), to the role he played in the circle of Lorenzo de Medici and the Platonic Academy at Florence, and to the attitudes expressed in his comic epic, the *Morgante Maggiore*, particularly through his highly unorthodox character, Astarotte.[5] Astarotte is also a demon, like Mephistopheles, and like him an engaging and witty personality, worlds remote from the un-mixed embodiment of evil which is the orthodox devil.

Pulci himself, with his cynical, free-thinking frankness and witty vulgarity, was a thorn in the flesh of the Florentine Platonists. He wrote some devastating lampoons mocking their lofty idealism, their ecstatic transcendentalism by which they winged their souls dizzily upward into the angelic spheres and came back with an exact knowledge of the un-knowable. In the epic Astarotte remarks that when he was a seraph, he had seen no such thing as Dionysius the Areo-pagite and Pope Gregory the Great report about the celestial hierarchies. Pulci's hilarious lampoon on Ficino's specula-tions as to the exact spot where the soul entered and left the body resembles Mephisto's witticisms on the same problem after the death of Faust.[6]

The great patron, Lorenzo the Magnificent, was a truly divided soul. On the one hand he joined wholeheartedly in the speculative flights of the Platonic Academy, indulging in its lofty cult of melancholy, and writing some of its most ex-pressive poetry, while on the other hand he wrote his free-spirited carnival songs (which Goethe was later to read with such admiration[7]), and relished Pulci's sharp, deflating jibes and his reduction of everything ideal to bemired absurdity. Matteo Franco reproached Lorenzo for his unholy attach-ment to Pulci, about which Lorenzo himself was restive. Everyone in the circle no doubt breathed a sigh of relief when that scoffer was no longer able to frequent the Medicean palace.

It is typical of Pulci's mockery and self-mockery that he put some of his most serious and lofty thoughts on divinity, cosmology, and the nature and destiny of man into the mouth of his fallen angel Astarotte—the whole subtly spiced with an ambivalent irony so that in many passages we cannot be quite sure whether he meant them to be taken seriously on the whole or as straight-faced parodies of philosophical discussions.[8] Astarotte has that same lambent, iridescent unpredictability and defiance of fixed categories with which Goethe endowed his Mephistopheles. We must be careful, however, not to push the analogy too far, since in many individual traits the two demons are quite different, and Pulci himself is in some ways a closer approximation to Mephistopheles than is his Astarotte.

The chief consideration, after all, is that a knowledge of Mephisto's broader Renaissance background would easily have resolved the long-standing uncertainty as to whether he came as an emissary from Hell or from the Earth Spirit or whether Goethe permitted in his drama two successive and mutually contradictory concepts from different periods of writing. There is no confusion of conflicting concepts; Mephistopheles is intended to be everything he is (regardless of any eighteenth- or nineteenth-century attempt at rigid classification); and he shows off the various facets of his complex character as the occasion or his personal whim turns them up, showing them now with startling honesty, now with a misleading twist, now with utter mendacity, at times even with a slight touch of decency and nobility. Throughout he plays with orthodox human concepts of what the devil ought to be like, his references to himself as a devil are characteristically made in a jesting tone, and he does take great delight in playing the devil on occasion. He is thoroughly diabolical at those critical points in the drama where he gives the action a twist to involve Faust deeply in crime. In the larger plan of things he performs certain necessary negative and deflationary functions on earth; with his all-pervasive impulse to vitiate every creative activity, to reduce cosmos back to chaos, he is a challenge and a stimulus to the constructive forces in man, the foil by which man learns about himself and his world. In this sense he is indeed equally the son of chaos and the servant of the Earth Spirit. And he will forever defy any exclusive classification, quite in accord with the spirit of the times out of which he arose.[9]

Mephistopheles for some of his most evil moments may have inherited traits from a Shakespearean character, Iago, though the entirely different background and motivation has helped to obscure the likeness. Once this vicious companion of Othello is well launched on his course, we can observe in him a striking prototype in his cynically clever twisting and wrecking of human relations round about him, his calculated employment of human weakness toward the increase of chaos, his ruthless involvement of everybody near him in the general destruction, and also his unholy glee at his success and at the helplessness of his victims who are forced unwittingly into crime or into undeserved anguish and death. His high intelligence, nimble imagination, and mordant wit, combined with his remorseless calculation and vicious nihilism, make him a villain with a more refined and terrible kind of infernality than that of the orthodox devil of folk literature, who belongs by comparison to a lesser criminal class. Even the duel between Valentin and Faust may represent in part a rearrangement of similar motifs from the duel in *Othello* between Cassio and Roderigo, where Iago, like Mephistopheles, cleverly managing the encounter from the shadows, helps bring it to its infamous conclusion.

However, the specific analogies are minor matters; the main point of comparison is that Goethe and Shakespeare, in different ways, have succeeded in showing with divine impersonality (and compassion) how calculating evil can involve a truly great and good though fallible man in tragic guilt, and cause him to bring upon the object of his tenderest affection piteous fear and mortal agony.

Fortunately, we know just how Goethe intended Mephistopheles to be presented on the stage, for he personally coached young Carl Laroche—perhaps the greatest interpreter of the role in the nineteenth century—down to the last inflection and gesture. A spectator who saw him in the first Weimar performance in 1829 reported on him as follows: "He strictly obeyed the directions implicit in the poem, and remained throughout the humorously negating, wittily mocking, merrily skeptical, craftily spying spirit. In harmony with this were his gestures, his elegantly free deportment, his masterfully simple speech, which was neither strongly emphatic, nor pompously elevated, nor straining for effect, but always fluent, impressive, intelligible, and according to Hamlet's precept pronounced 'trippingly on the tongue.' His Mephistopheles was no devil of flesh and blood who roams about like a roaring lion seeking whom he may devour. It was a symbolic phenomenon standing at the pinnacle of the poem."[10]

Thus it is clear that those modern interpretations which accentuate the overtly diabolical in the figure of Mephistopheles represent a crude oversimplification and go contrary to the intent of the poet. This character in his appearance is, above all else, the elegant, accomplished villain of the Renaissance who carried out his nefarious designs with such grace, wit, and mockery, that he aroused admiration and even a perverse affection among his contemporaries. Underneath the appearance, of course, there lies depth beyond depth of the paradox of good and evil in human life. Goethe once called him "the living result of a great world view."[11]

The nature of the aerial spirits and their relations to Mephistopheles and to Faust should also become clearer when seen in the light of the easy informal attitude of the Renaissance toward the supernatural. The ideas concerning such spirits which were widely held in that age explain and confirm Goethe's intent, and are quite consistent with the interpretation resulting from a careful, comparative study of the pertinent passages in *Faust*. While the better-known, orthodox writers divided the spirits sharply into good and evil, the less orthodox allowed for almost every shade and gradation, and were especially fascinated by the middle spirits who were on the whole kind and good-natured, who could be very wise and helpful, but also whimsical, prankish and at times downright malicious. All this, of course, is a commonplace of folklore, though not of orthodox theology, and has remained a living tradition to the present day in fairy tale and fancy.

All through the Middle Ages the theologians tried in vain to stamp out the traditional belief in such natural spirits, particularly by claiming that they were actually evil spirits disguised to lead gullible mankind astray. But in such matters orthodoxy could not be enforced; the folk and the poets continued to cherish the richly varied figures of their imagination. In the Renaissance the more freely speculative writers combined the pagan elf and fairy lore of their own lands with the spirit lore of Graeco-Roman antiquity. As early as Hesiod certainly, and perhaps earlier in Orphic tradition we find the theological doctrine well established that the air is filled with "daemones" and "heroes," and that there is a hierarchy of other imbuing spirits in nature and the world.[12] The orthodox writers continued to condemn all such beliefs, whether classical or not, and to explain spirit manifestations as the works of the Devil.

In Goethe's drama, Wagner inclines to the orthodox point of view, Mephistopheles tries to claim "the little fellows" as his own, and Faust yearns to lift up his soul to the realms of the "heroes," the noble ancestors, and sends an invocation to the "daemones," the spirits of the air. In sum, we find in the drama a typical Renaissance syncretism of ancient and medieval concepts, similar, for instance, to that in Palingenius' popular *Zodiacus Vitae* which first appeared about 1531.

In common belief then, the aerial spirits are not bound by the obligations of either good or evil, as angels or devils are, nor do they have immortal souls to save, as men have. So

they float about freely on their missions of duty or fun, subject only to the laws of their nature, maintaining social con-
tacts both above and below. In *Faust* they get along quite
well with Mephistopheles, though they relish his discomfiture
when he is trapped by the pentagram. They are in the main
very kindly disposed toward men, tricky in small matters
just for fun, but not truly malicious for the most part. Because of their healing and restorative functions they are deeply
shocked at anything destructive, such as Faust's great curse:
thus their earnest adjuration that he reconstruct the world
he had destroyed, and Mephisto's nimble twisting of their
meaning following his offhand mendacity: "These are those
little fellows of mine" ("Dies sind die Kleinen von den
Meinen"). Their aversion to everything connected with destruction and death is a familiar article of folk belief, and
many stories report their audible song of lament at times of
human crisis and impending disaster.[13]

What the Renaissance thought of these aerial spirits is of
especial importance to us wherever relations to the "Faustian"
and "Mephistophelean" appear. Paracelsus conceived of them
as "elementals" and was apparently the first to call the in-
habitants of the element of air "sylphs." He is most emphatic
in opposing the orthodox theologians who denounce them as
diabolical spirits.[14] Agrippa also takes up the matter of the
aerial spirits, but more according to the convention of the
Graeco-Roman writers on such matters. In the third book
of his *De Occulta Philosophia*, he even divides the beings
intermediate between gods and men into "heroes" and "daemones," naturally without the slightest connotation of evil
attaching to the latter.[15] He connects this classical terminology with Northern myth and legend (Merlin's father, the
Alrunes, Odin, Thor, etc.). Like Paracelsus and others he considers the lowest order of spirits, those closest to man, to be
without immortal souls and subject to death, though endowed with superior wisdom in their own element and with

the gift of foreknowledge. In the first book, chapter 39, after his discussion of good and evil spirits, he clearly sets off a third kind, with whom the magus can establish contact: "Let no man, therefore, doubt that in like manner by some certain matters of the world, the gods of the world may be raised by us, or, at least, the ministering spirits, or servants of these gods, and, as Mercurius saith, the airy spirits (not supercelestial, but less high)."[16] In the spurious fourth book, which is often found appended to the other three, the neutral nature of these spirits, their generally favorable and beneficent attitude toward human beings is even more plainly stated.[17] Johann Valentin Andreae's imagined magus, Christian Rosenkreutz, while pursuing his philosophical studies at Damcar in Arabia, also communes with the elemental spirits ("elementarische Inwohner") and learns from them.[18]

From Paracelsus, Agrippa, and other sources, perhaps by way of Simon Maiolus and Heinrich Kornemann, came the novelistic treatment in Montfaucon de Villars' *Comte de Gabalis* of 1670, where the whole matter is treated in a playfully sophisticated and equivocal tone appropriate to the airy nature of the subject. However, Goethe need not have known either this or its Italian imitation in Gioseppe Francesco Borri's *La Chiave del Gabinetto* of 1681, for everything in them is derived from earlier authors and tales, ancient, medieval, and Renaissance. Besides, Goethe's great friend, Wieland, was an expert on all matters involving the middle realm of the free spirits. The narrative tone is also nothing new, but a few passages from Villars' tale are worth examining for their illuminating parallels and analogous attitudes.

The fictitious German count of the story, "whose lands lie toward the frontiers of Poland," was apparently modeled after the occult master Michael Sendivogius. He comes to Paris and reveals to the neophyte author that the spirit world is open to the wise, and that he too could be brought into direct communication with it. The spirits are creatures of the four elements (gnomes, sylphs, undines, and salamanders, in the Paracelsian terminology). The master offers elaborate refutations of the neophyte's orthodox belief that the spirits are demons from hell, by citing examples of their godliness and their good will toward men. He stoutly defends an unorthodox theological tenet according to which Satan and his hosts are bound in hell, cannot themselves come to man to tempt or molest him, but have alliances with certain neighboring elemental spirits of earth (gnomes) to perform such missions for them. Since the passage expounding this belief may help illuminate several facets of Mephistopheles' complex character and his position in the scheme of things, it is quoted here. The master is explaining that the Devil is the mortal enemy of the elemental creatures who seek for association with human beings in order to attain immortal souls:

The Devil is a mortal enemy, said the Comte, " 'especially of the Nymphs, Sylphs and Salamanders. As for the Gnomes, he does not hate them nearly so much because, as I believe you have already learned, the Gnomes, frightened by the howlings of the Devils which they hear in the centre of the earth, prefer to remain mortal rather than run the risk of being thus tormented should they acquire immortality. Thence it comes to pass that these Gnomes and the demons, their neighbors, have a good deal to do with one another. The latter persuade the Gnomes, who are naturally most friendly to man, that it is doing him a very great service and delivering him from great danger, to compel him to renounce his immortality. In exchange, they promise the man whom they can persuade to this renunciation that they will provide him with all the money he asks for, will avert the dangers which might threaten his life during a given period, or will grant any other condition pleasing to him who makes this wretched covenant. . . .'

" 'Then, Sir,' cried I, 'in your opinion these covenants, of which demonographers cite so many examples, are not made with the Devil at all?'

" 'No, assuredly not,' replied the Comte. 'Has not the Prince of the World been driven out? Is he not confined? Is he not bound? . . . He can do nothing against man. He can only inspire the Gnomes, his neighbors, to come and make these propositions. . . .' "[19]

Later the neophyte read the midnight sermon which the master had delivered to a group of recusant gnomes in an effort to convert them from their allegiance to the Devil.

Goethe, it would seem, conceived of Mephistopheles (of one aspect of him, at any rate) as an elemental spirit of the earth; for early and late, from the Gretchen tragedy of the *Urfaust* to the imperial battle of the fourth act of Part Two, he connected him in words, deeds, and ever recurrent allusions with things mineralogical and subterranean. From this point of view, the poet would be quite within the bounds of tradition when he whimsically contemplated for a time allowing this waggish miscreant of his to be saved in the end.[20] And more important, it is also traditionally correct (rather than confusedly inconsistent) to give such a figure that complex set of relations to chaos, hell, the mineral earth, the creative matrix, the aerial spirits, man, and God, which Goethe actually did give his Mephistopheles. He is a "demon," but not one who is separated by an unbridged chasm from the good spirits. Goethe restored the ancient graduated scale of the "daemones" which allowed for every transition stage from the negative pole of the malignantly destructive, through the mixed middle spirits, to the exalted tutelary geniuses of mankind at the upper positive pole. In his function Mephisto usually operates at the negative pole, but in his person he can associate with the middle spirits and even on occasion pay a visit to heaven.

There are also isolated and less important parallels in Villars indicative of a common tradition. There is the neophyte's

alarm when he thinks the master is about to summon the
spirits of the air; there is the equation of the gnomes with
homunculi (Homunculus calls Mephistopheles "cousin");
and there is the old and oft-told story of the sylph of un-
earthly beauty who has to leave her mortal lover when the
conditions of her stay are violated; she becomes disembodied,
leaving behind her only her earthly raiment.[21]

Pulci introduced such elemental aerial spirits into his epic
for comic purposes. Deriding the transcendental flights of
Ficino and the other Platonists, he has Astarotte claim that
they had been deceived by the "spiriti folletti," the elusive,
delusive creatures of the air who busily misinform and mis-
inspire such philosophers, though some of the other spirits
perform nobler and more useful functions:

> ". . . they are not bound
> In water or in glass, but dwell in air
> Showing deceit and falsehood everywhere.
>
> In company they journey boasting then
> That they have made what is not seem to be;
> Some take delight in making fools of men,
> Some find their pleasure in philosophy,
> Some bring hid treasures to the light again,
> Some tell false visions of futurity,
> And thus to you a courteous tale I tell
> For courtesy is present even in Hell."[22]

Reading John Dee's lengthy accounts of his converse with
spirits, one quickly notices their strangely mixed qualities.
However, the best description of such amoral, normally good-
natured, witty and wise, roguish and volatile creatures occurs in the last masterpiece of another and greater Englishman of those times, in Shakespeare's *Tempest*, in connection
with Ariel and the other merry sprites of the island. But we
should not pass over in silence the variegated assortment of

such beings in his earlier *Midsummer Night's Dream*, where both their prankishness in deluding mortals in harmless ways and their essential benevolence in all important matters is so ingratiatingly displayed. It is perfectly consistent, for aerial spirits, that they should aid Mephistopheles by putting Faust to sleep with a hypnotic song of sensuous allure, and then on the next day feelingly lament the destructive nihilism of his great curse. We can observe that Goethe himself consciously recognized their dual nature when we compare the summary sketch which he made for Part Two in 1816 with the conversation ten years later where he analyzed for Eckermann the attitude and function of the spirits in the opening scene of the second part.[23] In the one he emphasizes their delusiveness, in the other their healing benignancy. He did not change his mind between 1816 and 1826; aerial spirits simply are that way.

To return to the *Tempest*, it is probably not accidental that Shakespeare called his magician Prospero, which is a synonym for Faustus. Not only is Prospero very much like the worthy, handsome scholar-magician, John Dee, but what is far more significant, he may well have been intended by Shakespeare as an opposite figure to Marlowe's Dr. Faustus,[24] to show the benignant master of natural magic in intimate, controlling relation to all the forces of nature, good, middle, and evil. Here is the ideal picture of the Renaissance man of science who has succeeded in his quest for the inner meaning and pattern of cosmic movement, as Goethe's Faust has not at the opening of the drama. For the Renaissance scientist, to understand, to know, is to have control and power in that field of knowledge; to have penetrated to the vital center of the laws and acts of nature is to be the master of natural magic.

It would behoove us to de-emphasize the fancied and frail affinities of the magus Faust to the conjuror Dr. Faustus, for it is virtually out of the question that Goethe could have known Marlowe's drama in his youth. On the other hand, he certainly did know *The Tempest* by 1769,[25] and the figure of the magus Prospero is more likely than any bedeviled conjuror to have had a great and lasting appeal for him. The hermit in *Satyros* is a kind of Prospero who befriends a Caliban, with a similar return of gratitude; brought perilously close to death, his only regret is that his knowledge of nature should die with him: "Yet that alone grieves me, that I have sought out arduously the depths of Nature's lore, and now in vain; alas! that man's exalted science, many an occult force, should vanish with my spirit from the earth."[26]

In Goethe's charming musical drama *Lila* of 1777, the wise physician, Verazio, assumes the role of a magus who shows traits of Friar Laurence in *Romeo and Juliet* and more especially of Prospero. He too associates with benignant spirits like those in *The Tempest* or in *Midsummer Night's Dream*. The obvious parallel that both Faust and Prospero abjure magic in the end has always been recognized. It is also not at all a new thought that the protagonist of the *Urfaust* and the magic to which he resorts need to be understood in terms of Prospero and his magic and should not be interpreted in terms of Dr. Faustus and his conjuring; but it is a thought which, if heeded, might avert some common misconceptions.

This has brought us to Goethe's protagonist and his problems as they are unfolded in the first monologue.

CHAPTER III

FAUST'S INTELLECTUAL POSITION:
CUSANUS, PICO DELLA MIRANDOLA,
AND OTHERS

HE FIRST MONOLOGUE OF FAUST, with what follows, is a very complex matter, and we must naturally keep in mind when examining parallels and sources that Goethe here as elsewhere was no simple borrower. He was a creative artist who at a highly inspired, synthesizing moment drew together a multifarious web of threads into a unique texture. Some of the most distinctive, character-giving threads are clearly discernible as coming over from the Renaissance and it should be of value to describe and trace them, particularly if they will help us to avoid some long-standing misinterpretations.

The very first lines, the survey of the four university faculties, the "Fakultätenschau," are an old standard feature of the Faust drama, in a general way similar to the opening of Marlowe's tragedy and, vaguely, of the German puppet play. But looking deeper into the origins, we perceive that Goethe's lines have a more intimate organic connection with what follows in the drama than has ever been realized.

More than a century before Marlowe's *Dr. Faustus* there is a disparaging survey of the academic faculties to be found in German poetic literature, and what is more important, in a context of some significance to our inquiry. This passage occurs in a poem by Hans Rosenplüt, "Von dem müssiggener" (the idler), of about mid-fifteenth century. A few brief excerpts will indicate its trend and purpose:

"The Lord of Hell has never made more captives than among the idle and slothful, and when the sinner falls into despair; on these two flanks he catches the most with his snare for souls, with all his spirits. . . .

"If I had learned in all the schools and were a doctor of medicine, and of theology no less, and were a lofty philosopher, and a proved physician . . . and had served my three years of practice, I should even so not know remedies as well as when a worker sweats a drop while he grows warm at his work. . . .

"Therefore work is the most godly order which has ever been established on earth. . . . So never let yourself be found idle, even though despair stays away. . . ."[1]

Significant is the setting of this survey of the faculties in a poem stressing the sinister sequential relation of idleness (sloth), melancholy, and despair, their culmination in paralysis of the will, in surrender to evil, and on the other hand, salvation from this danger in work, in ceaseless activity, which will cure man of doubt and despair better than will the learning of the faculties. This train of thought is characteristic of the newly rising attitudes toward life, and we find every motif of it, freed from its religious matrix, running through *Faust*, including the motif of "Care," of "Sorge," first appearing in the monologue after Wagner's interruption and then again toward the end of the second part. Dürer's engraving, "Melencolia I," as we have learned to understand it in recent decades, will also illustrate various aspects of this interrelation.[2]

The separate elements of the poem, like those of the engraving, come largely from medieval tradition, as does so much of the Renaissance; the self-assertion of plowman and craftsman, for instance, dates from the strong movement in the previous century. The newness lies in the special combination and evaluation, the developing secular point of view, and the trend toward a new standard of human dignity and validity. The layman, not the monk, belongs to the most divinely instituted order. It is easy for a modern reader to underestimate the significance of the poem; the seemingly trivial exposition of the fourfold course of sweat, for instance, is actually of some importance in connection with a memorable passage in another work of Goethe's.

It is characteristic of the Renaissance that Dürer's engraving and Rosenplüt's poem do not stop with the depiction of the vanity of human skill and knowledge (the arts and sciences) and with the depiction of the despairing surrender of man in the face of this futility. Out of the depths of melancholy there is a vista into the future, a solution of the dilemma. In the poem it is the simple old Christian solution of steadfast faith and hard work. In the engraving the further vista is suggested by the parable of perspective, for with consummate irony a large part of the city below is framed in the rungs of the ladder. All is relative and mutable; the given point of view of any one moment is in itself illusory. Like everything else, the despair will pass, the wings will recover from their leaden fatigue and carry the human genius onward again; the temporarily exhausted greyhound will run again with the swiftness of thought; and above all, the genius of a new generation, the putto playfully manipulating the serious tools of the mind, will grow up to carry on with a new vitality. True, at the depicted moment of crisis both Dürer's and Goethe's protagonists (the latter after one further trial) feel that this is the end, there is no more beyond; but the creating artist from his superior perspective knows that this seemingly final stage is, like everything in life, only a transitional stage and, what is more, he indicates that plainly.

Naturally, Rosenplüt's poem, when lifted out of the symbolic setting of its age and regarded from a modern point of view, carries little conviction as a parallel to the Faust monologue. However, it is not necessary to go into an elaborate elucidation of the poem and it would indeed be wrong to weigh it down with too much bearing on the monologue. Dürer's engraving is closer in symbol and outlook, though it lacks the survey of the faculties; such a survey is implicit or explicit in a great variety of Renaissance works, most elaborately and impressively in Agrippa's treatise on the incertitude and vanity of the sciences and arts. And yet, the old-fashioned poem serves well as a point of departure for our inquiry.

In the poem the learning of the faculties is contrasted unfavorably in its efficacy with the drops of sweat of a farmer or craftsman which in a fourfold manner aid him on his way to God. This reminds us at once of the contrast emphasized again and again by Nicolaus Cusanus (1401-1464); and, oddly enough, this poem may just possibly be the first modest poetic echo of the great German cardinal's foundation work of Renaissance thought.

As the expositor of his principle of "docta ignorantia" Cusanus in several dialogues chooses the "Ydiota," the layman, without formal learning but with a wisdom that springs from his sure grip on realities. To this man with the practical wisdom of experience comes the erudite scholar who has searched widely through books, despairingly, without finding what he most desired. The scholar now begins to realize that the straightforward, practical ways of the layman have brought deeper, truer insights into the essentials than have his own scholastic methods. Cusanus in his "Ydiota" clearly and definitely sets up the ideal of a new layman's knowledge. The Layman undertakes to convince the Orator (that is, the humanist) as well as the Philosopher (the scholastic) of his ignorance; he puts into question the fundamental presuppositions of the humanistic as well as of the scholastic concept of knowledge. As Cassirer points out,[3] Cusanus becomes the champion not of declining scholasticism, not of rising humanism, but of a third specifically modern way of thinking which takes as its point of departure concrete technical, artistic problems, the phenomena of actuality, and subjects them to a deeper consideration and the application of principles and theories. The inference was: away from book learning, whether scholastic or humanistic, on toward knowledge of life by practice and experience.

Leonardo da Vinci and Leon Battista Alberti were the great followers of Cusanus in this tendency. The English editor of Leonardo's notebooks, Edward McCurdy, has already in two stimulating, though in part dubitable, pages drawn the parallel between this genius and Goethe's Faust and has outlined the correspondence which he believes to exist between the two parts of the drama and the two phases of Leonardo's life: "The personality as represented in the early biographies is substantially that which is expressed in the phrase of Michelet, 'Léonard, ce frère italien de Faust.' It tells of him that he chose rather to know than to be, and that curiosity led him within the forbidden portals!"[4]

Though we cannot follow McCurdy in many of his opinions on the *Faust* drama, his interpretation of the dominant drive and increasing purpose of Leonardo reveals unmistakably the "Faustianism" of a Renaissance personality with whom Goethe must have been acquainted since early youth and to whom he later devoted extensive and fruitful study. The great hydraulic and irrigation works of Leonardo in Lombardy, his harbor work at Cività Vecchia, and near the very end of his life the project of the great canal to connect the Loire and Saône represent a fittingly "Faustian" culmination of his life. However, as we shall see in the next chapter, there is another renowned Renaissaance artist who can perhaps serve even better as a prototype.

Faust's condemnation both of the old established learning represented by the four faculties and of the new humanist learning of textual criticism and rhetorical adornment represented by Wagner, his turn from these to nature, to inner feeling, to experience for guidance—all this can be found in a continuous Renaissance tradition from Nicolaus Cusanus onward. Gerard Dorn, in the preface to his commentaries of 1584 on the *Archidoxa* of Paracelsus, conveniently exemplifies this attitude by his advocacy of the third way to knowledge through nature and his condemnation of both scholasticism and humanism. It was never a broadly popular tradition, not nearly as prevalent as humanism proper, but it was a highly select tradition of a thin line of great and greatest men: Leonardo, Alberti, Pico della Mirandola, Paracelsus, Telesio, Giordano Bruno, Tommaso Campanella, Francis Bacon, Johann Kepler, Joachim Jungius, Johann Valentin Andreae, Samuel Hartlib.

Even more closely akin to Goethe's *Faust* is the philosophy of Giovanni Pico della Mirandola who, as Cassirer has shown,[5] built his whole work upon the threefold basis of his master Cusanus: the principle of learned ignorance ("docta ignorantia"), the principle of the coincidence of opposites ("coincidentia oppositorum"), and the symbolic knowledge of God (these we shall consider later). To summarize the relevant lines of thought: Pico's point of departure is the principle of man's freedom, that no predetermined place in the universe has been assigned to man, that he is completely free to sink or rise in the scale of being. No material determinism can have a decisive effect on his spirit, but only his own self-determination. With this completely open range for self-realization, man is the Proteus, the eternally mutable; and that is no longer his shame, as it was in earlier times, but his glory: he can develop his own individuality and attain to his highest potentialities. He must do so independently, whatever the dangers of free choice may be.

Pico expresses this in his famous "Oration on the Dignity of Man" by having God address the newly created Adam thus: "Neither a fixed abode nor a form that is thine alone nor any function peculiar to thyself have We given thee, Adam, to the end that according to thy longing and according to thy judgment thou mayest have and possess what abode, what form, and what functions thou thyself shalt desire. The nature of all other beings is limited and constrained within the bounds of laws prescribed by Us. Thou, constrained by no limits, in accordance with thine own free will, in whose hands We have placed thee, shalt ordain for thyself the limits of thy nature. We have set thee at the world's center that thou mayest from thence more easily observe whatever is in the world. We have made thee neither of heaven nor of earth, neither mortal nor immortal, so that with freedom of choice and with honor, as though the maker and molder of thyself, thou mayest fashion thyself in whatever shape thou shalt prefer. Thou shalt have the power to degenerate into the lower forms of life, which are brutish. Thou shalt have the power, out of thy soul's judgment, to be reborn into the higher forms, which are divine."[6]

The way of a free man should naturally be upward. As Pico expressed it: "Let a certain holy ambition invade our souls, so that, not content with the mediocre, we shall pant after the highest and (since we may if we wish) toil with all our strength to obtain it." The mind of man can be satisfied with no moderation, indeed with no possession of any sort that has fixed limits. On the way upward man will inevitably slip, fall into sin and error; that is a necessary corollary to his striving. In good as in evil man is never a completed being, he never rests securely in good nor is ever a hopeless prey to sin.

Nature for Pico has as its chief characteristic a universal vitalism. Nature forms a single great interconnecting Life, with a continuous chain of effects and an all-suffusing power of sympathy. As he says: Magic "is nothing else than the utter perfection of natural philosophy. . . . Abounding in the loftiest mysteries, [it] embraces the deepest contemplations of the most secret things, and at last the knowledge of all nature. . . . [This magic] having more searchingly examined into the harmony of the universe, which the Greeks with greater significance call συμπάθεια, and having clearly perceived the reciprocal affinity of natures, and applying to each single thing the suitable and peculiar inducements (which are called the ἴυγγες of the magicians) brings forth into the open the miracles concealed in the recesses of the world, in the depths of nature, and in the storehouses and mysteries of God, just as if she herself were their maker. . . ."

And yet, all our knowledge is at best a knowledge of fragmentary and scattered phenomena, and from the Many we can never by a process of synthesis arrive at a comprehension of the One, of God, of ultimate truth. Pico sees the Many rather as expressions, as images, as symbols of the One. That is symbolic knowledge; our thinking and conceiving, in so far as it is directed toward the divine, can never be an adequate perception, but only an image and a metaphor.

To conclude the summary entirely in Cassirer's words: "This idea, that man is his own maker and moulder, adds a new element to the basic religious notion of 'likeness to God.' For it is no longer God who in his creation once and for all impressed upon man his own seal, and created him after his own image. The likeness and resemblance to God is not a gift bestowed on man to begin with, but an achievement for him to work out: it is *to be brought about* by man himself. Just this ability to bring it about, rooted in his own nature, is the highest gift he owes to the Divine grace. . . .

"Upon the angels and the heavenly intelligences their nature and their perfection have been bestowed from the beginning of creation: man possesses his perfection only as he achieves it for himself independently and on the basis of a free decision.

"And this challenge stands not only for single individuals, it stands also for historical epochs. From each epoch to the next there is handed down a definite intellectual heritage; an uninterrupted chain of tradition binds the present to the past. It would be presumptuous and disastrous, according to

Pico, to seek to break this *'aurea catena'* which binds together all times and all intellectual and moral life. But on the other hand each moment of history can and must be taken and interpreted as a new beginning and a fresh start. For without this meaning the basic principle of human freedom would be infringed. . . .

"The freedom of man consists in the uninterrupted creativity he exercises upon himself, which can at no point come to a complete cessation. . . . He must be forever seeking and choosing his own path: and this choice carries with it for him a perpetual danger. But this uncertainty, this perpetual peril of human existence—not in the physical, but in the moral and religious sense—at the same time constitutes for Pico man's real greatness. Without it he would not be what his destiny demands he should be.

"Man's failure is hence for Pico not merely guilt; it is rather the expression of that same indestructible power that makes it possible for him to attain good. Only a being capable of, and as it were at the mercy of, sin can achieve that highest worth that lies in the independent overcoming of sensuality, in the free elevation to the 'Intelligible.' "

This then may serve as an extract of those lines of thought which have the closest relation to the Goethean Faust. Pico here outlines the kind of human being that the Lord predicates in the "Prologue in Heaven" and that Faust exemplifies in his earthly course. But it was not until the brilliant analysis published in 1942, that these noble elements of his thought were extracted from the large matrix of his works and were seen to give it character and coherence. Just how effectively the main structural lines of his philosophy were concealed can be seen in most of the earlier critical studies. Anyone reading them would fail to receive a clear notion of his philosophy and, what is more, would be thoroughly discouraged from turning to his writings for light on anything. There are few instances where the nineteenth and

early twentieth-century misunderstanding of the Renaissance is more clearly discernible. If no *Faust* scholar saw
the pertinence of Pico to his studies (except in the special
matter of magic), it is for the reason that Pico's thought
was simply not readily accessible and there was nothing
that pointed toward it. In his own time, by contrast, the
main purpose of the brilliant young nobleman was well
understood, and it was neatly epitomized in his appellation,
"Count of Concordia."

It is possible that Cassirer, perhaps unwittingly, learned
from Goethe how to see what was central about these early
Renaissance philosophers from Cusanus onward. That is
not to suggest for one moment that with insufficient evidence he imputed to them ways of thinking which were in
reality Goethean; he was able to support his interpretation
at every crucial point by direct quotation, and was too careful a scholar to be led astray by subjective background memories. However, the intuitive sureness with which Goethe
found the vital center, making it the nucleus of his own creation, while forgetting the non-essentials and perhaps even
the particular source, this may well have been a guide for
Cassirer through the labyrinth of Renaissance philosophy and
may have in part caused him to bring out with particular care
just those trains of thought which Goethe also felt to be of
greatest importance for modern man and which he endowed
with poetic life in his masterpiece.

CHAPTER IV

THE DIVERSITY OF RENAISSANCE
PROTOTYPES AND MOTIFS

ESPITE THE CLOSE AFFINITY of the two, we ought not to jump to the conclusion that Pico is *the* source for Goethe's *Faust*. It would be regrettable if we were haunted for the next fifty or even five years with the spirit of Pico, as we have been for the past fifty with the spirits of sundry critical favorites, worthy and unworthy. The scope of his relevance to *Faust* is, of course, as broad as that of any favorite; nevertheless, his many points of contact with the ways of thinking and attitudes on human destiny expressed in Goethe's drama are not unique in the Renaissance, they are characteristic. He was simply among the first to build upon the new philosophical foundations of Nicolaus Cusanus and to describe articulately the new "Faustian" man, freely striving and erring, freely determining his own destiny, by intellectual insight coming into sympathy with and control over the forces of nature, putting his emphasis always not on the avoidance of error but on the overcoming of error.

Other men of the Renaissance *lived* according to these fundamental principles, to a greater or lesser degree; though they did not always express themselves as articulately and completely, their works and course of life are often exemplary illustrations. In a different way from Leonardo, Michelangelo exhibits certain "Faustian" tendencies, in his life, in his painting and sculpture, and in his sonnets: the essential goodness and knowledge of the right way, despite all-too-human and constant erring, the melancholy and despair together with the restless dynamism and overreaching impatience, the continuous self-development with its transcendence of past selves and

46

transition to new spheres of higher activity, despite all adverse circumstances. Since Goethe's response was far stronger to living phenomena than to abstract formulations, it is indeed more likely than not that much of his concept of Faust came from exemplars such as Michelangelo rather than from expositors such as Pico.

It only adds to the greatness and truth of the work that Faust is as imperfect, fallible, sinful, reprehensible as Michelangelo was throughout his earthly pilgrimage even to the extremities of his old age. Neither of them are paragons of virtue to adorn a moral tale for a schoolboy text. That has at times caused Faust to be rejected by some who maintain that such a representative figure should either have been more ideally formed or that the author should have indicated his repudiation of him plainly and unmistakably; certainly God should not have committed the shocking indiscretion of translating that disturbing old reprobate into heaven. Essentially, the complaint of the moralists and abstractionists is that the poet failed to make his protagonist conform to the demands of the German ethical and philosophical idealism of his age. They do not realize that he did not intend or wish to do so, that his work rests on entirely different premises.

Goethe did not have in mind any abstract idealistic representative of Western man purely striving onward and upward, such as Kant, Schiller, or the Romantic philosophers and poets might have schematically projected. No one has a right to be disappointed that Faust was not modeled after such an impossible ideal, however elevating and moralistically soothing it may be. Goethe intended him to be otherwise: a flesh-and-blood man of passionate energy and uncheckable drive toward a succession of goals, the meaningful pattern of which becomes gradually clearer only as the end approaches. The poet learned especially from Renaissance exemplars such as Michelangelo—with his almost frightening vitality—what were the tragic implications of the restless, relentless quest for ultimates in truth, beauty, insight, and comprehension. The human shortcomings of the man, and also the shortcomings of the world around him which is content with much less, and is resentful and obstructive toward the man who wants much more—both conspire to create great wreckage and suffering along his thorny path.

Goethe rightly called his drama a tragedy; the drama of a genius is usually tragic. There is genuine guilt, for a genius is not and should not be above the moral law, as superficial admirers of the "Faustian" may wish to assume. But there is also genuine achievement, a noble transcendence of the care and despair of human shortcomings, an ultimate clarity on the problem of human purpose and destiny. With that comes the divine grace which removes the last earthly imperfections and completes the redemption of a great soul. The ancients understood this and symbolized it in the apotheosis of human, fallible, heroic Hercules. The Renaissance understood this when it never for a moment disparaged a great work because of the all-too-fallible nature of its achiever. Goethe understood this when he created the Faust he did rather than the type which his age called for and many a critic since has desired. There are doubtless increasingly many in our times who also understand this and are willing to take the man as the poet gave him to us, without addition or detraction, and without interpretation contrary to the clearly stated intention.

Albrecht Dürer too in his life, art, and writings could have furnished some of the traits and motifs for the Goethean Faust. Indeed, there is a continuous line from the later fifteenth century until well into the seventeenth both of prototypes for the character and of possible sources for the ideas and circumstances of the drama. True, many of the separate traits, ideas, and attitudes are very ancient, coming together from all cultural regions and from all periods of human history. But the point is, they *came together*, came together first in the Renaissance to form that peculiar synthesis which Pico soon formulated philosophically and Goethe centuries later incorporated poetically—each in a great act of fusion and conciliation. For Pico the heritage of man could not and should not be limited to classical antiquity, as it was for the humanists proper; for him the Middle Ages were fully as precious; he looked to the wisdom of the Egyptians, the Persians, the Jews, and the Arabs, as well as to the wisdom of the Greeks and the Christian West.[1] Alberti too, and many another, was free of the humanist bias that the classics alone were worthy of study and imitation. As Campanella expressed the broader perspective symbolically in his fifty-second sonnet:

> "Six thousand years or more on earth I've been:
> Witness those histories of nations dead,
> Which for our age I have illustrated
> In philosophic volumes, scene by scene."[2]

Goethe in the same spirit made the whole outline of the second part of *Faust* the hero's voyage through space and time back to the origins of Mediterranean civilization (in the figure of the Homunculus back to the origins of life itself in the littoral sea), and forward again through Homeric Greece, the Germanic migrations, the high Middle Ages, on through the eighteenth and nineteenth centuries, to the future in a new land. What the poet here presented implicitly, he stated explicitly about the middle portion, the Helena drama, in letters to several friends. On October 22, 1826, he wrote to Wilhelm von Humboldt: ". . . it now plays over a full three thousand years from the fall of Troy to the capture of Missolounghi. Thus this too can be considered a unity of time, in a higher sense."[3] It is significant that Goethe's poetical version of this Renaissance ideal of synthesis and perspective should occur in the *West-Östlicher Divan*:

> "He who lacks the inward treasure
> Of three thousand mastered years,

Must stay in darkness, without measure,
Live from day to day in fears."[4]

In Campanella's sonnets there are a number of other utterances also characteristic of the "Faustian": the first sonnet on the penetration to the innermost secrets of nature, the abandonment of the fragmentary and merely verbal knowledge of the schools, the fourth on the poet's unstilled intellectual hunger, the fifth on nature as a book, and so on.

There is a remarkable sonnet by Luigi Tansillo (1510-1568) which presents the aspirations of his love so purely in terms of the Platonic flight, that Giordano Bruno in his dialogue, *Gli Eroici Furori*, was able to include it (spoken by Tansillo, though with some changes) as a perfect expression of the philosophical flight of human aspiration. In *Faust* the sonnet is re-echoed in such varied passages as the defiance of the Earth Spirit, the facing of suicide, the yearning for flight (toward the end of the Easter Walk), and the Euphorion tragedy:

"Now that these wings to speed my wish ascend,
   The more I feel vast air beneath my feet,
   The more toward boundless air on pinions fleet,
Spurning the earth, soaring to heaven, I tend:
Nor makes them stoop their flight the direful end
Of Daedal's son; but upward still they beat:
What life the while with my life can compete,
Though dead to earth at last I shall descend?

My own heart's voice in the void air I hear:
Where wilt thou bear me, O rash man? Recall
Thy daring will! This boldness waits on fear!
Dread not, I answer, that tremendous fall:
Strike through the clouds, and smile when death is near,
If death so glorious be our doom at all!"[5]

Bruno himself in life and thought had many "Faustian" attributes, as has already been recognized. Torquato Tasso, whom Goethe knew and loved from childhood, also wrote a sonnet on the same general theme, in his "L'alma vaga di luce e di bellezza," but with the significant additional feature of the attracting power of the earthly eros. The lack of an English translation is offset by an Elizabethan sonnet which in part derives from it, namely the seventy-second sonnet in Edmund Spenser's *Amoretti*:

"Oft when my spirit doth spread her bolder wings,
In mind to mount up to the purest sky:
It down is weighed with thought of earthly things
And clogged with burden of mortality,
Where when that sovereign beauty it doth spy,
Resembling heaven's glory in her light:
Drawn with sweet pleasure's bait, it back doth fly,
And unto heaven forgets her former flight.

There my frail fancy fed with full delight,
Doth bathe in bliss and mantleth most at ease:
Ne thinks of other heaven, but how it might
Her heart's desire with most contentment please.
Heart need not wish none other happiness,
But here on earth to have such heaven's bliss."[6]

A distinctively Renaissance note here in Tasso and Spenser is their equable treatment of the two opposing tendencies within the soul of man. There is no scorn or condemnation of the earthly as opposed to the heavenly love, but instead, a recognition of the rights of both, and of the healthy normal talent of man for making the earthly symbolize the heavenly and fuse with it. Faust's similarly equable and objective treatment of his soul dilemma needs to be understood from this Renaissance point of view; there is a struggle, but it is not the simple traditional one between good and evil, as has been too easily assumed.

To pass over the other varied affinities, one of the most significant as well as persistent motifs that occurs in the drama, in a wide range of mood and expression, is the motif of flight. Indeed this has the same importance and symbolic value in *Faust* that it has in the Renaissance and its higher endeavors, whether in Pico or in the numerous poems like the two just quoted, whether as sublimation, as mystic symbol, as wish-fulfillment, or in Leonardo's "inventions," or in the cruder, very ancient form of demon-aided flight (the last sometimes for a noble purpose, as in Pulci).

On the more prosaic, though still imaginative side, the life and works of the physician-scientist, Hieronymus Cardanus, are rich in suggestive parallels to Faust, far beyond the concept of magic as the intuitive coming into harmony with the forces of nature. These have not been explored, even though Goethe's later preoccupation with Cardanus is well known. The first record we have is in the summer of 1777 when Goethe read his brilliant, provocative autobiography. He must have been impressed by its remarkable portrayal of a first-rate mind and personality, no doubt also with its distinguished Latin prose, for he read it again the following year "with great enjoyment and sympathy," as he wrote to Frau von Stein. Whether he knew him earlier has not been ascertained but later he read the *De Subtilitate* and perhaps other works. What is more, he paid conscious literary tribute by fashioning the opening of his own autobiography after that of Cardanus', though characteristically transforming it with his whimsical, luminous humor.[7]

When Goethe included a short section on him in the historical part of his *Farbenlehre*, he was inevitably reminded of two other great masters of autobiographical frankness in the Renaissance, Benvenuto Cellini and Michel de Montaigne, especially of the former who was of the same age and was likewise of a highly problematic and enigmatic character. "Cardanus belongs among those men whom later times never finish discussing, about whom they do not easily come to an agreement. . . . He knew his own disposition up to a certain degree, but to extreme age he could not become master of it. Very often in connection with him, his environment, and his striving we have been reminded of Cellini, all the more since they were contemporaries."[8]

The next sentences, with their brilliant aperçu on the relation of Renaissance and Reformation to the new type of personal self-expression, do not specifically concern us here. However, Goethe's long occupation with Cellini from the mid-1790's onward does have its peculiar bearing on the further development of *Faust*, though certainly not on its inception or its intrinsic plan. Letters of his in 1798 and 1826 indicate that the most famous section of the artist's autobiography describing the long agonizing course of events from the genesis to the completion of "Perseus with the head of Medusa" became for the poet a symbol of his own long travail on *Faust*.[9] But far more to our purpose are the notes that he added to his translation of the autobiography, in an appendix on Cellini's times, his contemporaries, environment, art practice, personality, and works.

It would, of course, never occur to him or to anyone else to equate Cellini with Faust, but that he saw certain important resemblances between the two becomes reasonably clear from the following passages of section twelve, the delineation of Cellini. Goethe had just been sketching Medicean Florence: "In such an active city, at such an important time appeared a man who may be considered as representative of his century and perhaps as representative of the whole of humanity. Such personalities can be regarded as spiritual fuglemen who with vehement gestures indicate to us that which is, in very truth, inscribed in every human breast, though often only in weak and dimly discernible lines.

"What strikes us most vividly about his whole story, however, is the general quality of human character, so decidedly expressed, the instantaneous lively reaction when something opposes his being or his will."

"However, just as human nature is always obliged to fashion and manifest itself completely, even so does there appear in our hero as well as in his environment in this turbulent sensual world an ethical and religious striving, the ethical striving in greatest conflict with his passionate nature, the religious striving in comfort for inescapable suffering, deserved or undeserved.

"The picture of ethical perfection as something unattainable is constantly hovering before the eyes of our hero. Even as he demands outward respect from others, so does he demand inward respect from himself."

"The doctrine of his church no less than his times, so full of pressures and premonitions, drove him to the marvelous [the supernatural]."

"With a firm belief in a direct relation to a divine and spiritual world, in which we may hope to perceive the future in advance, he had to pay homage to the miraculous signs in which the universe, otherwise so taciturn, seems to express its interest in the fates of extraordinary men. . . .

"But his wondrous destiny brought him into relation not alone with the higher powers; passion and exuberance also brought him into contact with the spirits of Hell."[10] There follows a reference to Cellini's attempts at sorcery and to that traditional haunt of sorcerers, the mountains of Norcia between the Sabine country and the duchy of Spoleto—a locale which Goethe kept in mind and referred to in Act IV, in the last year of his work on *Faust*.

Not all of this is equally applicable to Faust, but the fraternal resemblance, or better the resemblance of contemporaneity, is unmistakable. Goethe clearly recognized attributes in Cellini with which he had endowed his own Faust, and the association of the two in his mind may have affected the further development of the drama. In the preceding section ten, on the Medicis, his reference to Cosimo's attitude toward Neoplatonism, for instance, contains a minor but clear verbal reminiscence of *Faust*.[11] Once more, however, to avoid being misunderstood, I should state that Goethe almost certainly never saw the Cellini-Faust relation as anything more than a parallelism, limited to a few interesting points, and that beyond this the few ascertainable direct influences from Cellini are of a peripheral nature. And yet, the glimpses we get of the poet's own reactions to aspects of the "Faustian" are not without value. He made his work on Cellini contribute also to the continuation of his great task.

Turning once more from the Italian to the Northern Renaissance, we can pass over with brief mention the far more important and intrinsic relations of *Faust* to Paracelsus since these have been explored in great detail though sometimes not with sufficient critical caution. On the other hand again, the parallels to Henricus Cornelius Agrippa von Nettesheim have been studied with less detail and adequacy.[12] Agrippa's three main works: on the vanity of all knowledge, on the occult philosophy, and on the excellence of woman, even the titles of them alone, symbolize three of the stages of Faust's course of development, and are surely more significant than the biographical detail of Agrippa's sinister black poodle which is generally mentioned in the commentaries at the proper line of text. The Paracelsians of the later sixteenth century also deserve closer scrutiny; the few references to them in this study may serve to indicate their considerable value in the elucidation of the drama.

John Dee, as has already been suggested, parallels Faust in even larger patterns and closer detail. When he was about to resort to magic, he wrote his apologia in his journal in the form of an invocation to God: "And forasmuch as for many yeres, in many places, far and nere, in many bokes and sundry languages, I have wrought and studyed, and with sundry men conferred, and with my owne reasonable discourse Laboured, whereby to fynde or get some ynkling, glimpse, or beame, of such the aforesaid radicall truthes. . . . Seeing I was sufficiently taught and confirmed that this wisdome could not be come by at mans hand, or by human powre, but onely from thee (O God) mediately or immediately. And having allwayes a great regarde and care to beware of the filthy abuse of such as willingly and wittingly did invocate and consult (in divers sorte) Spirituall Creatures of the damned sort: Angels of darknes, forgers and patrons of lies and untruths; I did fly unto thee by harty prayer, full oft, and in sundry manners. . . ." And he hoped that God would send good spirits to instruct him, though mentioning that he had been visited by evil spirits against his will.[13]

There was another, later Englishman, or rather Anglo-American, whom Goethe himself mentioned in connection with his background reading at the inception of *Faust*. In the eighth book of his autobiography, in recounting his mystical-alchemical studies in 1768 to 1770 during his illness and convalescence at Frankfurt, he gives a brief list of some of the authors and books he studied. In the tenth book, telling of his association with Herder at Strassburg soon thereafter, in 1770 and 1771, he notes that he concealed from his sarcastic mentor his three most cherished imaginative conceptions: his incipient plans for *Götz* and *Faust*, and his "mystic-cabalistic chemistry."[14] Of the authors and books he mentions (Paracelsus, Basilius Valentinus, van Helmont, Starkey, Welling, the *Aurea Catena Homeri*, Gottfried Arnold and Boerhaave), all are well known to *Faust* scholars and have been diligently scrutinized for sources and analogies, with one partial and one complete exception: Boerhaave and Starkey. The one is so well known that negative results rather than lack of investigation may account for his general omission. The neglect of Starkey, however, has been so complete that in summaries of this passage by the critics and commentators his name is frequently dropped, and in no case have I seen more than the epithet "goldmaker," the year of his death, and the remark that Welling cited him under the name of "Philaletha."

How unjust this neglect is, I hope to show more fully on another occasion. Suffice it to say here that George Stirk or Starkey (1628-1665) was born and spent his childhood in Bermuda, was educated at Harvard College, practiced medicine a few years in Boston, and about 1650 or 1651 embarked upon his colorful European career, the most sensational part of which is that he was apparently the author and certainly the promulgator of the works of the mysterious American adept and citizen of the world, Eirenaeus Philalethes, renowned all over Europe and very likely read by young Goethe. One passage of importance to us occurs in the autobiographical introduction of his work, *Natures Explication and Helmonts Vindication*, of 1657, which describes his course of disillusionment with book learning: ". . . at length Aristotles Logick I exchanged for that of Ramus, and found my self as empty as before: and for Authors in Medicine, Fernelius and Sennertus, were those I most chiefly applyed my self to, and Galen, Fuchsius, Avicenna, and others I read, and with diligence noted . . . till practical experience taught me, that what I had learned was of no value."[15] Then Starkey turned to Paracelsus and experiment (his form of magic and nature), later adding van Helmont as a guide. Interestingly enough, this "Faustian" course of travail took place about 1646 to 1648 in Cambridge and Boston, Massachusetts, with the assistance of the second John Winthrop's library which was well stocked with Neoplatonic, Hermetic, magical, and Rosicrucian volumes. This may, therefore, be a slight Anglo-American influence at the very inception of *Faust—*

even as the concept of a free people on a free soil of Faust's last earthly activity was (as Hohlfeld has so beautifully shown) a great English and American influence at the culmination of the drama.[16]

It would be possible to go on through a list of about fifty names of Renaissance men who in their persons or writings display important parallels to Faust.[17] We can assume with some certainty that Goethe, despite his wide range of reading, would have been unacquainted with some of the names on such a list. Where there are so many to choose from, the question of specific prototypes comes to be of less importance than the general prevalence of "Faustian" phenomena by which the Renaissance is established as the spiritual and actual home of Faust.

With this superabundance of parallels and possible sources the eighteenth century cannot in any way compete. Its few analogues tend to be of limited scope and applicability, only rarely shedding any significant light on the larger issues of the drama. By contrast, the many analogues from the Renaissance become all the more impressive when we observe that they frequently offer pertinent and applicable explanations of crucial problems in *Faust* and, what is more, reveal previously hidden lines of unity among its various parts.

 HEN FAUST on that critical night contemplated his intellectual impasse and turned from the learning of the faculties, he had already investigated another way to knowledge which the Renaissance scholar considered traversable, albeit dangerous. He resolved to embark upon it:

> "Wherefore I've given myself to magic
> In hope through spirit voice and might
> Secrets now veiled to bring to light . . .
> So that I may perceive whatever holds
> The world together in its inmost folds,
> Its germs, productive powers explore,
> And rummage in empty words no more."[1]

From Shakespeare's Prospero, as well as from Agrippa, Dee, and others we have already learned unmistakably what kind of magic Faust turned to, and what part the spirit world plays in it. For one of the sharpest contrasts between the divine magic of nature on the one hand, and diabolical conjuration on the other, one can read section 32 and following of Pico's "Oration on the Dignity of Man." Such a contrast, in more or less developed form, is a Renaissance commonplace, though severely censured by the dogmatic theologians. In Pico, as in most of the other writers, the operation of true natural magic depends on the principle of correspondences and sympathies between man, the microcosm, and the totality of nature, the macrocosm. The magus who attains a true understanding of the inner forces and connections of nature thereby also learns how to manipulate and control them.

It must be clearly understood that Faust's going over to magic implies his going over to nature. Therefore, the words that immediately follow, his apostrophe to the moon and his yearning to be with nature and the spirits of nature, do not represent a break in sequence but a perfect psychological continuity. He turns in revulsion from academic learning and from the equipment for it with which his study is stuffed; he turns with a last hope and expectation to the wide land of nature and to the book which is to guide him into it, namely "the mysterious book from Nostradamus' very hand." Thus the psychological circle is completed: the thought of magic leads Faust to the thought of nature, the thought of nature to the book of magic. Therewith he abandons the narrow confines of his study with its learned lumber, ironically saying of it,

"That is your world! That's called a world!"

alluding, of course, to the miserable showing it makes over against the great world of nature, the macrocosm, which he hopes to enter with his chosen guide.

Some readers, who have not observed this relation, have been mightily disturbed that Faust, just after his ecstatic yearning for nature should turn to such a guide book and be diverted by it from disporting himself amid the beauties of the moonlit night. As always, however, Goethe knew what he was about, and the misinterpretations (this one and also the more subtle ones) rest to a large extent on a misunderstanding of the word "nature" as it is here used. One should not lightly assume that the nature Faust yearns for and turns to is the Rousseauian, romantic, sentimental nature of flowers, birds, bees, scenic landscapes, springtime, young love, and dewy grass in the morning—the nature that imbues the conventional poetry of the eighteenth and nineteenth centuries.

If we do assume this, the monologue becomes afflicted with disturbing discrepancies and discontinuities, though, of course, Goethe scholars have long since abandoned the monstrous exegesis of the nineteenth century which reduced the monologue to a group of disjointed fragments composed at various times.

Actually it should be quite clear and unmistakable what Goethe meant by "nature" in this first monologue, not only from the tight linkage of magic, nature, book of Nostradamus, macrocosm, and Earth Spirit, but even from the descriptive adjectives and associations that accompany his use of the word. From the five references to "nature" we know that the poet here envisions her as a living being furnishing the environment for man, as the teacher of man, the unfolder of the powers of his soul, and the revealer to him of the colloquy of spirits. Her symbol, the sign of the macrocosm, reveals her forces round about, and its graphic lines show her actively creative before the soul's eye of the magus. But intellectual vision is no substitute for direct intimate contact, and the references to nature culminate in Faust's yearning address to her as the great mother, the all-nourisher, of whose breasts he finds himself deprived while languishing in vain.[2] This is the nature which was traditional from remote antiquity through the Middle Ages, and was particularly elaborated in the Renaissance; it is the great nature sought with equal fervor by philosopher, scientist, magus, and poet; it is not the limited nature of landscape beauty for transcendentalists, aesthetes, and vacationists.

Before we turn to answering the question why Faust chose as his guide a book by Nostradamus (of all people), let us see what he found in the book. He first opened it to the sign of the macrocosm, and then to the sign of the Earth Spirit. It was therefore obviously a book with valid, magically potent symbolic representations of great nature, the macrocosm, and of its subsidiary parts with their tutelary spirits, perhaps including also the symbols of the planets, of the four elements and the fifth essence, and representations of the complex of emanations by which the Neoplatonic cosmos was connected in a unit of interacting forces. From the colorful description of the sign of the macrocosm we should be more inclined to think of these representations not as dry schematic linear diagrams, but as magnificent, inspiring pictorial delineations.

Was there any such book or attempt at a book of which young Goethe could have had knowledge? Certainly neither Swedenborg nor Herder, who are at times mentioned in this connection, ever wrote a book containing vivid inspiring representations, or even dull outlines, of either macrocosm or Earth Spirit. The oft-mentioned six-pointed star, composed of two triangles, or the meager diagram of the macrocosm in the *Aurea Catena Homeri* is quite inadequate for calling forth Faust's vision with its impassioned poetic utterance. More seriously to be considered is the Jacob's ladder, a favorite subject in art, of which Goethe from boyhood onward must have seen many an example, especially among the illustrations of Biblical works which were often highly detailed and imaginative. The Jacob's ladder does at any rate show "How heavenly powers ascend, descend," even though it does not at all match the rest of Faust's vision and does not really have even this one feature in a macrocosmic setting. It is true that the younger van Helmont (Francis Mercurius) did use it in that cosmic setting (as Bruno did before him, be it added, and no doubt others). And yet, there is not the slightest evidence that Faust seeing the heavenly powers ascending and descending envisioned any kind of a ladder-like arrangement. It has simply been taken for granted that there is no other choice, that this must be the picture intended, even though the image of the next line, "Each unto each the golden vessels giving," cannot possibly be, in actuality never was, combined with this iconographic tradition.

There is close-knit evidence, though indirect to be sure,

that young Goethe was well acquainted with an entirely different tradition of macrocosmic representation, a tradition, moreover, which is more appropriate to the Faust who has turned to magic and has opened the book to the great sign. We can begin with a good likelihood: that Goethe knew an author whose works were adorned with some of the most splendid and imaginative engraved representations of the macrocosm. That author was Robert Fludd (1574-1637). Though his name is never once mentioned in Goethe's works, diaries, or letters, the negative evidence, as so frequently, does not seem to be decisive. The poet's curiosity about this speculative scientist may first have been aroused in early youth by the description in Jacob Brucker's history of philosophy, or in Daniel Morhof's *Polyhistor*.[3]

That he subsequently turned to Fludd's works themselves and studied the engravings is demonstrated with fair (though not absolute) certainty by a later passage in *Faust*, which has puzzled the commentators. It occurs at the end of the Easter Walk, in Wagner's frightened description of the spirits of the disease-bearing winds. Only the vaguest kind of analogies have been found for this passage, and the opinion has been expressed that this "highly poetical" description was Goethe's own invention.[4] And yet, every detail of it is not only contained in a treatise by Robert Fludd, the *Medicina Catholica*, published at Frankfurt in 1629, but is illustrated in the accompanying engravings. Since there is no other known source for the passage and since this is a completely adequate and graphic parallel, we can, provisionally, admit it as the source.

References in Brucker, Morhof, and other known reading of young Goethe would almost surely have aroused his curiosity, and once he opened the Frankfurt and Oppenheim editions of Fludd's works, he could not help but be entranced by the remarkable folio engravings they contain. Again and again in almost every conceivable iconographic form these engravings attempt to set down a symbolic representation of the macrocosm: the stringed instrument running through the cosmos and indicating its harmonies and correspondences, the concatenation of the three realms of creation in all their hierarchical complexity, the more conventional though still highly imaginative depiction of the planetary and supraplanetary universe with its ministering angels, and so on through a number of variants.

None of the Fludd engravings that I have till now been able to examine correspond in detail to the cosmic spectacle that Faust describes, but they are incomparably closer to it than any previously advanced sources. With their sweeping imagination and soaring vision, these plates by de Bry and Merian are, in spirit, the graphic counterpart of Faust's poetic description, and we feel that we have entered the general area where the pictorial prototype might be sought. My further search for closer approximations in other Renaissance works was partly frustrated by the fact that there is a strange lack in even the greatest libraries in America of volumes containing plates of this nature, and this phase of *Faust* iconography can be satisfactorily studied only in one of the great old European libraries, since the nineteenth and early twentieth centuries scorned and neglected such matters. John Winthrop's library, brought to America three hundred years ago, is still outstanding even in its present fragmentary state.

One of the predecessors of Fludd was Heinrich Khunrath, whose *Amphitheatrvm Sapientiae Aeternae* was published in 1609 (a privately printed edition appeared in the preceding decade). John Dee and Johann Arndt admired it, and the latter wrote a special commentary on the illustrations. One of the engravings may well have stimulated Goethe's imagination for a scene in Part Two. However, the two representations of the macrocosm, the one depicting the descending chain of emanations, the other the ascending chain from chaos, through man, to the Godhead, are no closer to the imagery of Faust's sign than are the later ones of Mylius,

Fludd, and the few others that I have been able to examine. The Jacob's ladder, incidentally, does not appear in any of these.

Up to this point we have not found any close precedent for either Faust's vision of the macrocosm or for any book in which it was depicted; but we are in the proper environment, and after we have surveyed the necessary background, we shall find some good poetic prototypes. We may never find the perfect pictorial model which Goethe could simply have translated into his matchless poetry. Here he may have been, as so often, the creator of both content and form. We can, however, trace the materials that went into this creation far more clearly than they have been traced hitherto; and our finding of these materials will reveal Goethean connotations in this passage which have not always been clearly perceived, and will also guard us against other connotations that were never intended.

We shall see that Goethe was not the first to imagine such a book, and that some of the strange images he used were not original with him. Thus, three further steps which we can take will reveal to us something more of the young poet's imaginative and sovereign use of his materials. First a few preliminaries of background:

The tradition of this macrocosmic image is, to a large extent, Stoic and Neoplatonic though the origins of it go back much further to early Greek philosophy and Oriental speculation.[5] The picture of the circular motion of heavenly forces in the macrocosm uniting the superior with the inferior, bringing them into union and reciprocity, this picture is found not so purely and fully in the writings of the Neoplatonists as in the considerably earlier writings of the Middle Stoa and the Neo-Pythagoreans.

Closely related to the latter are the works attributed to the mythical teacher of the sciences, Hermes Trismegistus. The fabled *Emerald Tablet* of Hermes, mentioned by Goethe in

1770,[6] describes aphoristically the preparation of the quintessence, the philosophers' stone. It begins with the statement
that "whatsoever is above is the same as what is below, and
whatsoever is below is the same as what is above, so that the
miracles of the one thing may be performed." In the process of
preparation the material of the "one thing" to be perfected
"rises from the earth into the heavens and descends again to
the earth." This process is at the same time a symbolic cos-
mogony, for "thus was the world created." Here we have the
macrocosm, the reciprocity of heavenly powers; we could
even by a process of alchemical sophistry deduce the "golden
vessels" from this brief discourse with the aid of other ancient
alchemical texts, but there is no need to do so since the golden
vessels in a macrocosmic setting are not so completely absent
from pre-Goethean poetic literature as the silence of the
commentaries might lead us to believe.

It has been pointed out long since that in Manichaean belief the angels descend with golden vessels and other ceremonial equipment to bring the souls of the dead to heaven.
But certainly Faust does not envision either this or the more
general Manichaean process of the carrying up of the par-
ticles of light from this earth.[7] As a source or parallel it is
hardly closer than Aristophanes' poetic image of the clouds
"drawing up the waves of the Nile in golden urns."[8]

Much closer, both in imagery and setting, is a passage in one
of the great poems which Goethe knew and admired from
childhood. It is strange that this analogue should have been
completely overlooked, for it contains the picture of the stars
in cyclic motion fetching light in their golden urns. Not that
it is the perfect source by any means but it seems to be a dis-
tinct improvement on the analogues hitherto brought forward. In the seventh canto of Milton's *Paradise Lost* the
Archangel Raphael is describing to Adam the glories of
the six days of creation. On the fourth day God created the

heavenly bodies, concentrated the light in them, and with them set into motion the cyclic progress of time:

"Of light by far the greater part he took,
Transplanted from her cloudy shrine, and placed
In the sun's orb, made porous to receive
And drink the liquid light, firm to retain
Her gathered beams, great palace now of light.
Hither as to their fountain other stars
Repairing, in their golden urns draw light."[9]

Milton clearly conceived of the process as reciprocal, for earlier, in the fifth canto, he mentioned that the sun is nourished by the exhalations of the moon and the other planets:

"The sun that light imparts to all, receives
From all his alimental recompense. . . ."[10]

These ideas and images come from the same general area of Renaissance speculation from which came the macrocosmic systems of Fludd, Khunrath, and the rest. They derive ultimately from the natural philosophy of such Stoics as Posidonius.[11] The one permanently great contributor to the elaboration of the new vision of the world, with its unifying cosmic law was Johann Kepler, whose importance for the understanding of *Faust* will become sufficiently evident in the next chapter. Fludd was influenced by him (both of them influencing Milton in turn), and tried to rival him, especially in the delineation of the cosmic harmonies. Even more important for our present concern, Fludd gave himself with whole-souled devotion to another influence; and his imposing, intricate work on the greater and the lesser world, the *Utriusque Cosmi Historia*, may well have been conceived and developed in compensation for a great mysterious book which remained inaccessible to him, but which he fervently believed to exist.

Such a book never existed in reality but it had come to

imaginative life in the speculative circle around Christoph Besold (1577-1638), particularly in the inventive brain of young Johann Valentin Andreae (1586-1654). The stimulus was the ardent yearning for philosophical scientific unity in an expanding, perplexing universe. Instead of merely hoping for such a unity in the future, they created imaginatively the fiction that it already existed as the cherished treasure of a secret brotherhood founded by the ancient master, Christian Rosenkreutz. This wish-fulfillment Andreae incorporated in an account entitled *The Fame of the Fraternity of the Esteemed Order of the Rose-Cross,* which was intended only for private circulation in manuscript but was published about ten years later, in 1614, by someone who did not seem to know how it had originated.

According to this tract,[12] while Christian Rosenkreutz (1378-1484) was studying with the wise men of the philosophers' republic of Damcar (Damar) in Arabia, he translated into Latin the *Liber M* (the *M* no doubt standing for *Mundi, Macrocosmi,* or *Macrocosmi et Microcosmi*). The brotherhood of the Rose-Cross (the Rosicrucians) had subsequently devoted its philosophical-scientific efforts to revising and expanding the *Liber M.* One of the powers given by this book is the power of transcending the human limitations of space and time, an aspect of which (mentioned separately) is the power of foreknowledge, of prophecy, though this is humanly restricted and imperfect.

At the critical juncture of the world at this present time (that is, in 1604), the tomb of the master was found by a brother in the course of building repairs. The tomb itself was vaulted as a perfect philosophical model of the macrocosm, and on an altar in one of the recesses was found the model of the microcosm (the "minutus mundus").

In the account three parts of the *Liber M* are mentioned: the "Axiomata," the "Rotae mundi," and the "Proteus." The "Axiomata" presumably are the formulations of the universal cosmic laws ("What holds the world together in its inmost self"), the "Rotae" the astronomical chart of the motion of the heavenly bodies, of the changes of the world ("The stars' course then you'll understand"), and the "Proteus" the power of prophecy, or perhaps rather, the laws of metamorphosis and mutation.

If there is a closer approximation to the mysterious book which young Goethe imagined Faust as having, it has never been pointed out. And yet, Faust speaks of his book as being "from Nostradamus' very hand." Since Michael Nostradamus, a French Renaissance physician (1503-1566), is known only for his collection of hundreds of prophecies in verse quatrains (aside from a book on cosmetics and confections, and a few others attached to his name), the commentators have found the name incongruous at this point and generally agree that Goethe used it as a sonorous substitute rather than commit an even worse incongruity, an anachronism, by mentioning Swedenborg or Herder whom he really had in mind.

I could with equal or better reason claim that he really had Christian Rosenkreutz in mind, or the magi of Damcar, from whom came just such a book. Adding support to this hypothesis would be Andreae's remark that young Christian at Damcar listened to the converse of the elemental spirits ("how one spirit to another speaks") and learned from them; furthermore, the chief purpose of the Rosicrucian Fraternity was general reformation ("to improve and convert mankind"). Naturally, no kind of Rosicrucian reference could properly have been introduced into the monologue.

However, it would seem more reasonable to do Goethe the honor of assuming that he knew what he was doing: that when he wrote Nostradamus, he really meant Nostradamus. If we explore that possibility by turning directly to the seer's works, we shall find that the first two prophetic quatrains already give us the needed clue as to what Goethe intended to convey. It is odd that in this connection Nostradamus' own writings seem to have been neglected; only the reference works have been consulted, and there he is generally characterized as an astrological physician, with an even division between those who call attention to the startling fulfillment of his prophecies in the course of time and those who condemn him as a charlatan. The astrological pursuits will explain only one line: "The stars' course then you'll understand," but will not help us at all toward understanding his vital function in this context. We approach a solution when we notice that the first two quatrains, in which he describes his mystic union with the All, are not in the least astrological, they are classically Delphic. Even considered by themselves they are highly suggestive:

"Sitting by Night in my secret Study
Alone, resting upon the Brazen Stool,
A slight flame breaking forth out of that solitude,
Makes me utter what is not in vain to believe.

"With Rod in hand, set in the middle of the Branches,
With water I wet the Limb and the Foot,
In fear I writ, quaking in my sleeves,
Divine splendor! the Divine sitteth by."[13]

Even here on the surface there is the parallel to the lonely scholar in his study at night, the quaking terror and divine splendor of revelation, of making contact across the mysterious boundaries. It would take too long to explain the two quatrains in detail, especially the extraordinary double imagery of the second, nor is it necessary. For our present purpose we need only note that Nostradamus here indicates that he had succeeded in crossing the boundaries before which Faust stands baffled and frustrated, that he has successfully employed magic to penetrate to the inner core of nature's structure, from which he could transcend the material limits of time and space to foretell the future. His prefatory letter to his son, Caesar, describes how "this heat and Prophetical power draws near us" and man receives these secrets "by the subtle Spirit of fire," and his dedicatory letter to King Henry II mentions that he prophesied Delphically, "ex tripode oeneo."

For an explanation of this power of prophecy from the Renaissance point of view, we can most conveniently turn to the other great Florentine philosopher of the time of Lorenzo and Pico, the leader of the Platonic Academy, Marsilio Ficino (though Fludd's exposition would serve quite as well). Like many other Renaissance men, Ficino never questioned the possibility of foreseeing the future, and he offered what was to them a plausible scientific explanation of this phenomenon. His own mother (like Goethe's grandfather Textor) had foreseen the future so truly that for him it was an observed fact which simply required a reasonable interpretation. Modern analyses, such as in J. W. Dunne's *An Experiment with Time*, are basically not very different except for the added trimmings of the fourth dimension, of the newer time-space concepts. Dunne's book, incidentally, has excited the creative imagination of such very different writers as John Buchan and William Butler Yeats; it is the stuff of dreams that poems are made of. Ficino uses the ancient symbol of the three faces of time, past, present, and future, which are only partially visible to ordinary earth-bound man. He explains:

"The minds of all these [prophets] searched through many places and comprehended the three parts of time in one when they separated themselves from the body. . . . Or rather such a soul by its nature is almost everywhere and always. It is not obliged to go outside itself in order to look at many and distant places and to recall the whole past and to anticipate the future. Its achievements are won by leaving the body behind and by returning into itself, either because its nature is everywhere and always, as the Egyptians believe, or because when retiring into its own nature it is at once united with the divinity which includes all limits of places and times."[14]

This begins to make it clear why Goethe had Faust choose Nostradamus as a guide at this critical point: this seer by the succession of striking fulfillments of his prophecies was in the eyes of the late Renaissance (and after) the exemplar of the accomplished magus with a deep and sure knowledge of the inmost workings of nature, the magus who had managed to transcend the material bounds of time and space at will, who had gone beyond the confines of his individual self, and had established union with the world soul (Fludd's explanation) in which all time and space co-exist.

Furthermore, we can now see another close relation of this first scene of the *Urfaust* to the whole second part of the drama. Nostradamus by the use of the Delphic tripod and rod transcended the barriers of time into the future. Faust at first "transcends" to the timeless realm of the Mothers, and with key and tripod summons up the images of Helen and Paris (in popular belief, ancient and modern, the key was endowed with mystic qualities and was often used as a magic rod or wand; here it may symbolize the controlling and ordering light of reason in the realm of the creative imagination). Later he embarks upon his time-space voyage through human history, at first deep into the past, significantly with the Homunculus as his guide to begin with, then on his own initiative. Therewith he has likewise reached the highest stage attainable to the magus.

We know that this whole speculative realm was accessible to young Goethe and that in various ways he showed knowledge of it at the time of the *Urfaust* and later. As for "the three parts of time in one," for instance, he has his Prometheus state that he formerly served the gods, "because I believed that they saw the past, the future in the present."[15] This was the first of many comparable statements. A bit later, during his first year at Weimar, he repeatedly alluded to this mystery of time, principally in connection with the mystery of his love for Charlotte von Stein. As he wrote to Wieland in April, 1776: "The significance of this woman, the power she has over me, I cannot explain otherwise than by the transmigration of souls. Yes, we were once man and wife. Now we recognize each other, dimly as through a veil, in spirit mist. I have no name for us: the past, the future, the All." These last phrases especially indicate that he was clearly and consciously acquainted with the speculative literature on the transcendence of time in the world soul, the All. Well known is his poem of about the same date to Charlotte: "Why did you [Fate] give us these deep insights to view our future so presentiently? . . . Ah, you were in times of yore my sister or my spouse."[16]

Even in the pre-Weimar days it seems that he already had an imaginative concept of something like the realm of the Mothers, for he made playful use of one aspect of it in his exuberant skit, *Gods, Heroes, and Wieland* of 1774, when he had Alcestis and Admetus go to the grove across the Cocytus where "the animated forms of dreams can be viewed and heard."[17] Young Goethe's strangely blended sense of time is perhaps best expressed in the autobiographical account of his happy Rhineland journey in the summer of 1774: "One feeling, however, which strongly took possession of me and could not express itself wondrously enough, was the perception of past and present together in one: a way of looking at things which brought something spectral into the present. It is expressed in many of my larger and smaller works, and in a poem always has a benignant effect, even though at the moment when it comes to expression directly on life and in life itself, it must appear strange to everyone, inexplicable, perhaps unpleasant." His next words are: "Cologne was the place where antiquity could produce such an incalculable effect upon me." And he goes on to speak of the unfinished cathedral, the Jabach house and family portrait, and his recitation of "The King of Thule" and another new ballad of his.[18] He reacted similarly to the factor of place. It must be remembered that in the new Renaissance universe of Nicolaus Cusanus there is no center, there are no definite directions; upward and downward have no significance in reality; it is all a matter of point of view, of relativity. Goethe's description of the way to the Mothers is a poetic version of this concept of the cosmos:

> "Around them is no space, a time still less . . .
> . . . No way! To the Unexplorable,
> Never to be explored . . .
> Descend then! I could also tell you: Rise!
> It's all the same."[19]

This feeling of mergence remained with Goethe throughout his life, and he continued to express it poetically in his *Faust* and elsewhere. His symbolic play with time concepts is exemplified in the carnival scene in the first act of Part Two, where he has Euphorion appear as the Boy Charioteer before he was born in the third act. He enjoyed explaining this paradox to Eckermann: "Therein he [Euphorion] is like the spirits who are present everywhere and can appear at any hour."[20] In his letter to Nees von Esenbeck of May 25, 1827, he tells of his "three-thousand-year Helen" and his sixty years of imaginative development of this theme. During these years before its poetic fixation it was subject to the manifold mutations of developing in time until it was at last completed. "May it now finally endure as crystallized in the realm of time."[21] Helen and Troy, Byron and the Greek war of independence, and much in between, such as the victory of Don Juan of Austria at Lepanto, all are fused by Goethe in poetic synthesis.[22] The action of the whole of *Faust*, particularly of the second part, is virtually an exemplification of the time-space mystery.

Nostradamus is emphatically not the original and complete symbol out of which all this developed, on which all this depends; he is merely the initial symbol, but as such completely appropriate, once we see what Goethe intended and implied by naming him in the first monologue. He is, like Prospero, the accomplished master, a sure and sufficient guide into great nature. His gift of prophecy is only an outward sign of an inward grace. It identifies him as a man who has penetrated to the "radical truths" concerning the internal structure of the cosmos; he has communed with the spirits, has indeed had contact with the world spirit. The power of prophecy implies the conquest of space and time; the conquest of space and time symbolizes the transcendence of human limitations. That is what "Nostradamus" means at this point of the monologue, that is what he necessarily should mean in the context of the whole. But for the full reason why he was the best man to imagine here as the author of Faust's mysterious book, we need to advance a step or two further.

For the speculative mind of the Renaissance the name of Nostradamus was surrounded by an aura of connotations which would give him a place of very special importance. He was of Jewish descent, was well versed in astrology, in alchemy, and in the Greek mysteries, was a Christian, and lived in the anciently Celtic land of the Gauls. Therefore, he could be regarded as being in one person the great Renaissance master of the Mosaic-Cabalistic, the Chaldaic-astrological, the Egyptian-Hermetic, the Hellenic-Delphic, the Johannine-Apocalyptic, and the Druidic-divinatory mysteries—the incorporate synthesis of all the fragmentary traditions of occult knowledge which Pico had yearned to see united. What better man could young Goethe possibly have chosen as the author of Faust's book?

Nostradamus had himself learned from a volume that went far beyond those of the four faculties; he had learned from

the Book of Nature itself, to which so many Renaissance philosophers, Paracelsus, Bruno, Campanella, Figulus, exhorted
men to turn, to which Faust indeed did turn. And that brings
us to a final reason why Goethe may have chosen the name
of Nostradamus as the symbol of cosmic mastery. This reason depends on a typical Renaissance pun which those times
would have found natural and even illuminating, but which
our times might find difficult to accept without protest. However, I shall proceed, even at the risk of being taken too seriously and literally. Goethe must have known the atrocious
pun made on Nostradamus' name in the Latin epigram of a
contemporary because it is quoted in nearly every book that
contained an account of the man. It would therefore not be
surprising if Goethe were indulging in another, more appropriate pun which would offer a further signification, a
deepening of connotation. Nostradamus, that is Notre Dame,
means Our Lady.

Now to the Renaissance mind Our Lady would mean far
more than the Virgin Mary, the mother of God, it would
also mean her symbolic analogue, Mother Nature, whom
Faust in this monologue characterizes in specific emblematic
terms as *mater nutrix*. In the philosophical speculation of antiquity as well as of the Renaissance this process of syncretism
was a normal mental act: Venus, Isis, Demeter, various mythical women such as Leda and Danae, all were symbolically
equated with the divine "Physis," Dame Nature, who was im-
pregnated by Jove, by the sun, by the spirit of God. That
the Virgin Mary was placed in this symbolic complex is
indicated time and again in the painting and poetry of
the Renaissance, for instance in the altar piece of Piero
della Francesca where Virgin and Child are enthroned under the shell of Aphrodite and with the egg of Leda sus-
pended above Mary's head. If anyone in our century should
find this repugnant, it is only because he does not understand the process of sublimation already started by the Pla-

tonists, Stoics, and Neoplatonists who used the old myths as symbolic representations of cosmic phenomena.[23] The Orphic hymns are splendid examples of this. Even the Middle Ages, and especially the Renaissance took over this symbolism and thought it no offense to equate the divine mystery of the immaculate conception and birth of the Son of God with the likewise divine mystery of the solar radiance impregnating the earth and causing it to bring forth its abundance.

Within the framework then of this quite normal process of Renaissance thought, "this mysterious book from Nostradamus' very hand" could actually be the Book of Nature itself. This would indeed open up the starry universe and the realm of spirits. This would indeed contain both the sign of the macrocosm and the sign of the Earth Spirit. It may be difficult, if not impossible, for a modern mind to take such verbal analogies and speculative constructions in the same light-hearted spirit of acceptance that a Renaissance mind would, for which wit and wisdom were still synonymous. That Goethe could and did do so, we are coming to see more and more clearly as our understanding of his imagery and symbolism increases. However, it is not really of vital importance whether we accept these particular significations or not. The important point is the Renaissance image of nature, which will not only help make Faust's first monologue clearer and completely sequential but will also show forth its relation to later parts of the work and its true place in the whole.

CHAPTER VI

THE EARTH SPIRIT

HERE ARE TWO REASONS for the Earth Spirit's overwhelming effect upon Faust, both made clearer from our examination just completed. Theophilus de Garancières in his commentary on the second quatrain of Nostradamus thus explains the utter terror of the "vates" when the moment of revelation comes: "This quaking is the disposition which the good *Genius* causeth in Prophets, that they may be humbled, and not be puffed up with pride, when they come near the Majesty of God, as we read in *Daniel, St. John*, and the 4th of *Esdras*. . . . And because the Divine Spirit after he hath cast down those, to whom he will impart himself, doth afterwards quiet them. . . ."[1]

Added to that is the reason for the Earth Spirit's humiliating rejection of Faust at this time: Nostradamus (or Prospero, or any accomplished magus) possessed all the knowledge and mastery which enabled him to go beyond material · limits; Faust, on the contrary, impetuous and impatient as always, wished to attain to this knowledge and mastery by an act of transcendence, soon after he had turned to magic. Hardly had he arrived at the point of admission of utter ignorance where, according to Cusanus, his real introduction to divine wisdom could begin to develop, when he was already storming the gates and demanding ultimates. He was frustrated here and defeated, as again later, by an overpowering desire which had far outrun reason and contemplation; for he was unprepared in soul and mind, though not in courage and human dignity, for the apparition he summoned.

It is characteristic of Faust, however, that after having taken the wrong approach, disastrously, he set about with full mind and will to learn the right approach, and was successful, as we learn in the scene "Forest and Cavern." The two attempts to win Helen give us a parallel instance in the second part. If we keep this in mind, we can easily resolve the seeming contradictions which have been pointed out among the various passages dealing with the Earth Spirit.[2] There is no real need to assert that the second reference, at the time of the wager with Mephistopheles, indicates a change of intention on the part of the author. When Faust here declares that the great spirit has scorned him, that nature is closed to him, it is barely thirty-six hours since his overwhelming rejection and this is truly the state of affairs at the moment; whereas by the time of the scene, "Forest and Cavern," he has not only been transformed by love and now has a positive attitude toward mankind, he has also been residing for some time in intimate and unforced contact with nature, its creatures and its phenomena. Thus here the *opposite* statement about his relation to the spirit is *equally* true in its very different circumstances. Enough time has elapsed to show the spirit's real intention toward him, characteristically having a strong dash of ominous bitterness mingled with the great good. The two prose passages in the scene, "Gloomy Day," still dating from the first period of writing, also fit into the whole with essential consistency. It is only necessary to realize that consistency in *Faust* is not static, formalistic; it is dynamic, developmental.

Furthermore, the regular pattern of such acts of transcendence goes from high intensity and inspiration to a sudden slump of exhaustion at the superhuman effort, and eventually to a remembrance of the event as a high point in life. That young Goethe understood this pattern, he showed in an entirely different context when he discussed the Pentecostal experience of the disciples of Christ in his "Two Important Biblical Questions . . .": "The fullness of the holiest, deepest perception momentarily exalted man to an over-earthly being; he spoke the language of the spirits and out of the depths of the Godhead his tongue flamed forth life and light. On that height of perception no mortal can maintain himself. And yet for the disciples the remembrance of that moment must have vibrated with rapture through a whole lifetime. Who does not feel in his breast that he would ever after long to return to it again?"[3] It is completely true to occult tradition that Faust, even after the humiliating rejection, should be resentful rather than relieved at Wagner's interruption, and that he should later look back on his colloquy as a cherished experience.

As for the Earth Spirit himself, the usual references to the concepts of Paracelsus, Basilius Valentinus, and Giordano Bruno account for his nature and function with reasonable adequacy, though not for the manner and guise in which he appeared to Faust, nor for the conversation with him, nor for the scornful initial rejection of him. A striking eighteenth-century analogue has been found, though merely for his apparition; even that partial analogue turns out to be disappointing on closer scrutiny, and unrelated to the poet's own visual image.[4]

With all the attention that has been paid to the problem, it is surprising that Goethe's very definite indications as to how he himself envisioned the Earth Spirit have not been given due consideration and have not been traced back to their sources. Though his sketch depicting the apparition was made over thirty-five years later, it can be demonstrated from his known readings of the early 1770's that he probably had this same image in mind at the inception of the drama.

Between 1810 and 1812, Goethe made a few swift sketches of scenes for a contemplated performance of the first part of *Faust* at Weimar; on one of these he portrayed the Earth Spirit as an Olympian god, evidently Apollo. Later for the Berlin adaptation he suggested the majestic bearded figure of the Zeus of Otricoli.[5] Without knowledge of the sources, it could with some reason be maintained that his image of a flaming Olympian was a late concept, resulting from his classicism, and was far removed from his visual image when he wrote the scene in the 1770's. But there is evidence that the Olympian apparition was in his imagination from the first, and that it derived from sources containing such accompanying features as the moon veiling its light and the world being the living garment of God, which can be found in no other analogue hitherto noted. These sources also explain why he thought of the spirit sometimes as Apollonian, sometimes as Jovian. This again is not an inconsistency on his part, but a meaningful feature of a great tradition.

If we wish to find such a graphic pagan representation of the Earth Spirit, we should not seek it in Plotinus and the other all-too-abstract Neoplatonic philosophers; we need to go back several centuries earlier, to the classical poets themselves. On the other hand, we should not expect to find a fully developed concept of this spirit in antiquity for there were very good reasons why that could not come about until the Renaissance. But first of all, a few possible causes of misunderstanding should be cleared away. The Olympian original of the spirit must not be envisioned as a cool, serene marble of Praxiteles which calls forth reverent awe and aesthetic admiration in the beholder. This is a living god revealing himself, unveiled, in blinding radiance and terrible majesty. (In Stoic monism spirit was a refined and subtle kind of fire, of light, of life principle.) Such a direct revelation is all but unendurable; according to some ancient religions it is utterly unendurable. It is terrifying, it overwhelms the beholder. This, however, does not justify the grotesqueries of some modern stage performances. Goethe himself was later quite emphatic that there should be nothing grotesque or monstrous about the apparition.[6] That would be contrary to the Earth Spirit's own description of himself as a constructive functionary and servant of the Godhead who fabricates the world of phenomena, the concealing-revealing garment of God. There is an awesome aloofness and impartiality about him, a scornful contempt for human presumption, but nothing evil or sinister. He is essentially beneficent, like everything creative, as we can see even more unmistakably later in "Forest and Cavern."

It is necessary to stress this majesty and benevolence because there is another kind of Earth Spirit in antiquity of which Goethe certainly was aware. This is the evil "spirit of the world" of the New Testament and the church fathers, the bitter enemy of the Holy Ghost who is the Spirit of Heaven.[7] There can be no possible relation between that Earth Spirit and Goethe's, even as there is in *Faust* none of the grim dualism, none of the absolute antagonism between good and evil, none of the ascetic denial of this world that we find in primitive Christianity and in so many of its sister religions and philosophies at that time and since then. This is another obvious point that needs to be stressed because many things in the drama have been misunderstood through having been approached from this dualistic point of view. Actually, the wholly different environment of thought and imagination out of which the Earth Spirit originated likewise came over into the work and helped determine its character.

In attributes though not in scope, Goethe's Earth Spirit is very much like the world spirit or world soul of the Greek philosophers. Goethe was following tradition in regarding every spirit as part of the world soul and similar to it; and on the other hand, the ancient poets and thinkers often referred to the world spirit in his strictly earthly functions. Goethe as much as equated the two when, in his first brief outline for the whole of *Faust*, he referred to the Earth Spirit as the genius of the world and deeds, that is, the spirit of nature and history. This is virtually a paraphrase of the *Urfaust's* "In the tides of life, in action's storm."[8]

In Brucker's outline of philosophy and elsewhere the

young poet could read that Thales and Pythagoras believed the world to be full of spirits ("daemones" and "heroes"), and that according to the oldest Greek philosophers such spirits, which emanated from the Divine Being, were contained in the world spirit and constituted it; the world soul penetrated all, so that there was no part of the universe which did not have something divine about it; from it the other gods and daemones originated.[9] Such a synthesis of world spirit and the world of spirits Goethe also found in the ancient poets.

From the pre-Socratic thinkers onward, but particularly in Stoic circles, there was an attempt at a peaceful mutation and assimilation of the swarm of gods and cloud of myths by making them symbolic of the aspects and forces of nature in an essentially monotheistic system. Chrysippus, the early Stoic, already envisioned Zeus or Jupiter as the aether, that is, the fifth element (quintessence), the fiery heaven, the life force; this practically identifies him with the world spirit. From Posidonius and others this way of thought went over to Cicero's treatise on the nature of the gods; and in Cornutus' work, Zeus was called the soul of the universe because he was the cause of all living things.[10] Apollo, being the sun, that is, the divine fire in visible, elemental form, was thus one aspect of Zeus, of the world spirit. Another aspect, for example, was Athena, Minerva, the divine reason, who sprang full panoplied from the head of Zeus.

In astrology the various planets were given the names of gods, and each planetary sphere was conceived of as being moved by a god and therefore indicative of that god's effect on human destiny. The Neoplatonists brought astrology into the correlation, so that Plotinus equated Saturn with "nous" and Jupiter with "psyche," that is, the world spirit.[11] When in the late Renaissance it became possible to imagine the earth as another planet, it was only natural that a man under the spell of this Pythagorean-Platonic-Stoic complex of thought and symbolism should imagine our planet also as endowed with its own moving, working spirit. More of this later. The ancient speculative thinkers, when they thought of the earth as a living being, usually referred only to the world spirit as the pervading life force, and almost never postulated a separately identifiable spirit for the earth itself. In the early Renaissance, Cusanus, who imagined the earth as a living being, ascribed this idea to Plato.[12]

Young Goethe may well have known Aratus' famous poem, the *Phenomena* (quoted by St. Paul, imitated by Virgil) and Cleanthes' majestic "Hymn to Zeus," where related speculative trains of thought are given poetic form. But we can move from possibilities to probabilities by going on at once to his known reading, examining first a few instructive passages from Virgil and Ovid and then turning to one which may have had some importance in developing his visual concept of the Earth Spirit. The first Virgilian passage, from the fourth book of the *Georgics*, merely gives the picture of the cyclic course of life (though it has a bearing on certain lines of Goethean thought in the second part and in other works). Classical scholars agree that by "deus" Virgil here means the Pythagorean "anima mundi": "Led by such tokens and such instances, some have taught that the bees have received a share of the divine intelligence, and a draught of heavenly ether; for God, they say, pervades all things, earth and sea's expanse and heaven's depth: from Him the flocks and herds, men and beasts of every sort draw, each at birth, the slender stream of life; yea, unto Him all beings thereafter return and, when unmade, are restored; no place is there for death but, still quick, they fly unto the ranks of the stars and mount to the heavens aloft."[13]

The second passage, from the sixth book of the *Aeneid*, where the spirit of Anchises is talking to his son, is much closer to Goethe's concept: ". . . a spirit within sustains [the world]; and mind, pervading its members, sways the whole mass and mingles with its mighty frame. Thence [from the "anima mundi"] the race of man and beast, the life of winged things, and the strange shapes ocean bears beneath his glassy floor. Fiery is the vigour and divine the source of those life-seeds. . . ."[14]

In the fifteenth book of the *Metamorphoses*, Ovid presents Pythagoras as speaking directly, giving an extended exposition of his philosophy, of the eternal flow and change of things, of the permanence of life itself in an endlessly changing cycle of manifestation, "All things are changing; nothing dies" ("Omnia mutantur, nihil interit"). At one point when speaking about the transitoriness of volcanoes—transitory like all else on earth—he imagines a real earth spirit: "For if the earth is of the nature of an animal, living and having many breathing-holes which exhale flames, she can change her breathing-places and, as often as she shakes herself, can close up these and open other holes." This image, however, like the eighteenth-century one mentioned above, is so grotesque that no value at all can be attached to it as an analogue.

A part of the Goethean Earth Spirit's self-description, "Birth and the grave, An infinite sea" ("Geburt und Grab, Ein ewiges Meer") corresponds to the Pythagorean images of the ebb and flow of life: ". . . as wave is pushed on by wave, and as each wave as it comes is both pressed on and itself presses the wave in front, so time both flees and follows and is ever new"; or again, "What we call birth is but a beginning to be other than what one was before; and death is but cessation of a former state."[15] The picture of nature as being both womb and grave is, of course, common in Renaissance poetry, and familiar from Spenser, Shakespeare, and Milton, but not with such strong stress as here on the ceaseless cycle of life.

Though, as Goethe tells us in the tenth book of his autobiography,[16] his joy in his favorite poet, Ovid, was nearly spoiled by Herder at Strassburg, a number of details from the

Pythagorean part of this fifteenth book apparently remained or were refreshed in his memory and went over into the second part of *Faust* and elsewhere. With the obvious relevancy of the *Metamorphoses* to the second act, the "Classical Walpurgis Night," it is nothing short of amazing that Ovid is so consistently slighted in the commentaries. Here in the Pythagorean section alone we find not only such details as the mountain that suddenly arose out of the plain but also much of the conceptual background of what took place along the seashore: the endless proteanism and intertwining unity and continuity of all life. The number of references to Ovid throughout Goethe's works is unusually large, and even in such a late work as *Wilhelm Meisters Wanderjahre*, Ovid served as the inspiration for a poem.[17]

The classical poem, however, which equates Zeus or Jupiter with the world spirit is Cicero's on his consulship, from which he quoted at length in the first book of his *De Divinatione*. We know that Goethe had read this work about 1770 or 1771, for he made a number of excerpts from it in his *Ephemerides*, the notebook of his readings of that time;[18] but even aside from that definite proof, which we fortunately possess, we could be reasonably sure that young Goethe would have been greatly attracted just at that time to the curious matter of the *De Divinatione*. Here are the pertinent lines where Cicero describes his vision of the world spirit during his nocturnal vigil:

> "First of all, Jupiter, glowing with fire from regions celestial,
> Turns, and the whole of creation is filled with the light of his glory;
> And, though the vaults of aether eternal begird and confine him,
> Yet he, with spirit divine, ever searching the earth and the heavens,

Sounds to their innermost depths the thoughts and
    the actions of mortals.
When one has learned the motions and variant paths
    of the planets, . . .
Then will he know that *all* are controlled by an In-
    finite Wisdom. . . .
Then, of a sudden, the moon at her full was blotted
    from heaven—
Hidden her features resplendent. . . .
Then through the fruit-laden body of earth ran the
    shock of an earthquake."[19]

Of course, the setting of these verses is an entirely different
one, and at best they can be made to account for the apparition of the Earth Spirit and a few accompanying features,
the Virgilian lines accounting far better for his function.
Seneca also equates Jupiter with the world spirit, and Plutarch
speaks of him as a flaming spirit whose intrinsic nature is
usually hidden under various forms: "Your Lord Zeus, is he
not, so long as he preserves his own nature, one great continuous fire?"[20]

But more important than these, there is a curious passage
about a certain Alexander Epicureus, who is supposed to have
lived about the time of Plutarch: "Alexander the Epicurean
held, that God was matter, or was not different from it, and
that all things were essentially God, and that forms were
imaginary accidents, and had no real entity, and therefore
he said all things were substantially the same; and this God
he called sometimes Jupiter, sometimes Apollo, and sometimes Pallas: and that forms were the Robe of Pallas, and
garment of Jupiter; and he asserted that none of the wise
men could fully reveal what was concealed under the robe
of Pallas, and the garment of Jupiter."[21]

This passage has been known and cited in connection with
Faust for its image of the world being the garment of the

Godhead. Now, however, together with the passage from Cicero and the others, it at once attains a larger scope of reference to the scene. Since it is quoted in a work that young Goethe likewise excerpted in his *Ephemerides*, we have some reason for believing that it and the Cicero together were influential in forming Goethe's imaginative picture of the Earth Spirit. If this is so, we have one further instance where young Goethe and old Goethe were assumed to differ but were actually in agreement. It should be noted that the passage containing Alexander's views is not isolated, but that it is possible to adduce parallels for every feature of it, especially from the Stoic philosophy, from the second book of Cicero's *On the Nature of the Gods*, for instance. Plutarch also speaks of Apollo as "Cosmos," the world spirit; and the image of the visible world being the garment of God (even of matter being divine) can be found in some phases of Alexandrian philosophy, also in the *Zohar*, and in various subsequent works such as those of Fludd.[22]

Though these ancient sources and analogues may have advanced our understanding of the appearance and the function of the Earth Spirit, as Goethe imagined him, they have no answer to other problems which this scene presents. Neither they nor any of the previously proposed sources can, for instance, be made to account for the conversation between the spirit and Faust (all the apparitions so far cited being completely mute). Two Renaissance tracts will take us another step on our way, particularly in the matter of the spirit's attitude toward Faust and the tone of his conversation. Even so, a number of problems remain unsolved.

The first tract is the pseudo-Paracelsian "Revelation of the Secret Spirit," otherwise called "The Book of the Apocalypse of Hermes concerning the Supreme Secret of the World," which was written about 1560 or perhaps earlier. In conformity with the Stoic tradition, as outlined above, this noteworthy tract equates the world soul or "anima mundi" with the fifth being or "quintessence," the most rarefied, spirit-like manifestation of matter, which is also the moving spirit of matter, a spirit that "appears" in a glorified and illumined body: "This spirit is called by Avicenna the soul of the world. For just as the soul moves all the limbs of the body, so this spirit moves all bodies; and as the soul is in all the limbs of the body, so this spirit is in all beings created from the elements. . . .

"This spirit is the secret hidden from the beginning . . . who lives fiery in the air and draws the realm of earth with it toward heaven. . . . This spirit flies through the midst of the heavens like a spreading morning cloud, leads its burning fire in water and has its clarified earth in the heavens."[23]

In other words, the world soul has in it the spirit of the four elements with their mutations one into the other. Perhaps it is significant in this connection that Goethe likewise definitely associates the approach of the Earth Spirit with the stirring of the other three elements, air, fire, and water. In Faust's description:

> "Clouds gather over me—
> The moon conceals her light—
> The lamp fades out!
> Mists rise—red beams dart forth
> Around my head—there floats
> A shudder downward from the vaulting
> And seizes me!"[24]

The author of the "Revelation" adds the warning: "Therefore thou shalt have no converse with this spirit until thou understandest it sufficiently." In the next paragraph he states: "This spiritual substance is neither heavenly nor hellish, but an airy, pure, and glorious body, and the formed medium between the highest and lowest. . . ." Thus the quintessence is conceived of as being the most sublime material manifestation of the world spirit.

The second treatise, with more and closer points of reference, is the "Dialogue between the Spirit of Mercury and the Monk, Brother Albert Beyer," first printed in 1604, though dated (falsely?) 1560.[25] There is, of course, a model in antiquity for such a dialogue between a questing philosopher and an informing spirit, namely, the *Poemander* of the legendary Hermes Trismegistus.[26] This earlier dialogue, too, shows interesting though rather general affinities to *Faust*; there are such features as the yearning for essential truth, the luminous apparition of Poemander to Hermes, the latter's mixed reactions of joy and trembling, the belief in a living interacting cosmos suffused by the world spirit, the world of phenomena seen as a beautiful picture of God, and finally, the double nature of man, earthly and heavenly, without any prejudice against the earthly but rather with approval of the loving commingling of the two.

In the Renaissance dialogue, which develops in an entirely different way, we at once notice the tone of lofty scorn with which the planetary spirit addresses Brother Albert, referring contemptuously to his conjuring hocus-pocus which actually had no effect at all in summoning him. Upon the monk's question as to whether he was a good or an evil spirit, he answers: "I am neither a good nor an evil spirit, but am one of the seven planetary spirits who rule middle nature, to whom is given the rule of the four different parts of the whole world." Though he remains aloof throughout, he does not in the end reject the monk but, on the contrary, consents to answer some of his questions and promises to return when summoned for good cause.

For an alchemist the Spirit of Mercury was naturally the one to summon; for the Goethean Faust the only planetary spirit that could induct him into the secrets of nature was the spirit of his own planet. Albert's concluding remarks on why he summoned the spirit offer some points of comparison: ". . . this vision appeared to me and held the aforementioned dialogue with me after I had stayed awake and gone to bed day and night with philosophical books and prayed God the Lord day and night with fervent sighs that He would in His mercy reveal the truth of this art to me. After I had worked in vain in the laboratory with my abbot for twenty-three years with great effort . . . ; I did in my ignorance (God forgive me), because I thought not otherwise than that one could learn the great secret from no man, but would have to force it from the spirits. . . . Then I say, on the aforementioned day through the usual ceremonies and accustomed conjurations . . . I summoned the Spirit of Mercury and requested converse with him."

This, like the passage from Dee, demonstrates that the Renaissance magus was superstitiously misrepresented by the orthodox, as in the Faust book, and that Goethe restored him to his true status as a deeply devout man who, after long vain labor, resorts to magic to establish contact not with evil spirits but with neutral (or good) spirits. Dee's experiences, as well as the solemn warnings that the Spirit of Mercury gives to Brother Albert against continuing his conjuring practices, illustrate very well, as does Faust's experience, how the more evil spirits can manage to insinuate themselves if such magical desires and practices are continued. Faust, like Prospero, in the end reaches the stage of wisdom where he realizes that magic had best be put aside even though it is used for beneficent purposes. Both magi make this great renunciation and leave themselves exposed to chance and the elements.

It would be highly gratifying if, after all these partial analogies, we could find a work in which there is a real Earth Spirit in an even more broadly "Faustian" context, a work in which, also, the whole long classical tradition is taken over and developed to a new stage. If we remember that most of the classical passages cited are ultimately Pythagorean and Stoic in background, we are well on our way toward finding the desired author and work. During the Renaissance (or more strictly speaking, during the transition to the Baroque) the greatest of the Pythagoreans did indeed most elaborately develop not only the image of the harmonic macrocosm, but also the image of the Earth Spirit. I refer to Johann Kepler (1571-1630) and to his famous though seldom read masterpiece, the *Harmonices Mundi* of 1619. In the concluding seventh chapter of the fourth book, the idea of the Earth Spirit ("anima terrae" or "anima telluris") is elaborated in intricate functional relation to the author's cosmology. Such a fully developed concept could come only in the post-Copernican period when the earth could be envisioned as one of the planets subject to their laws of movement and their kind of spiritual moving force. On the other hand, it had to come fairly soon, before the poetry of dynamics and harmonics was replaced by the prose of mechanics.

Kepler's references in the *Harmonices* show that he had also discussed the Earth Soul in previous works: especially in his *Epitome Astronomiae Copernicanae* of 1618, also in his *De Stella Nova in Pede Serpentarii* of 1606, and in his *Dioptrice* of 1611. Furthermore, his references to his readings in Plato, Virgil, Proclus, Pico, and others demonstrate once more the manifold continuity of this tradition.[27] It should be added that in his *Ad Vitellionem Paralipomena* of 1604 we can observe that one of the subsidiary sources of his concept of the Earth Spirit was Plutarch's dialogue, "Of the Face which Appears on the Orb of the Moon," chapter fifteen, where in a most elaborate and fantastic fashion the analogy is drawn between the universe and man's body, the macrocosm and microcosm.[28]

Kepler's exposition of the "anima mundi" and then of the "anima terrae" in the long chapter of the *Harmonices* is too complex for brief quotation or summary at this point. Interesting is the sequence: the soul of the macrocosm, the soul of the earth. Plainer and briefer is his treatment in the *Epitome* of the preceding year, or in his earlier German references to the matter, or in his summary of this phase of the *Harmonices* in his letter to Vincentius Blanchus of March 13, 1619. Florianus Crusius, in his letter of October 13, 1619, seems to prefer the word "spiritus" to "anima," at one point directly discussing the "mutationem operationum animae sive spiritus terreni."[29] Kepler also in his German dialogue with Dr. Röslin of 1609 uses both "soul" and "spirit" interchangeably, though in his Latin works he avoids the latter term in connection with the Earth Spirit, probably because of its ambiguity (and because of Platonic usage). In speaking of the aerial and other spirits in a German tract, he uses the word "Geister."[30] A few concluding sentences from the dialogue with Dr. Röslin will serve as a good brief summary, though for the fullness of relations and connotations one should turn to the *Epitome*, or best of all to the *Harmonices*.

In the dialogue, Kepler has just conceded that if Aristotle were right that the earth is dead matter, one would have to admit an external force of propulsion (compare Goethe's poem, "Was wär' ein Gott, der nur von aussen stiesse"). He continues:

"However, my reasons, as stated above, first of all posit a soul in the earth which has sovereignty of action over its body, that is, over the globe. . . .

"*D. Röslin*: This spirit, from my point of view, however, has to go through the whole world, is not peculiar to the earth, but is aetherial in origin.

"*Kepler*: I also allow for such a general spirit in my book, but alongside this one I have a special one for the globe of the earth, and demonstrate him through his functions, just related and otherwise."[31]

Here then is a genuine Earth Spirit, clearly and carefully distinguished from the world spirit. Furthermore, in the *Harmonices* and other works of Kepler we at last find the Earth Spirit in a congruent setting. The song of the arch-

angels in the "Prologue in Heaven" reminds us of the main
theme of Kepler's book: the demonstration of the universality of the laws of harmonic relations, specifically in the music
of the spheres (the "Brudersphären Wettgesang"). Such details are suggested as the glorious light-music of the sun and
the grandiose stormy progress of the earth planet revolving
turbulently through day and night, with its ebb and flood,
amid the calm serenity of God's space.

Kepler, like the Faust of the first monologue, passionately
desired to know "what holds the world together in its inmost
self," and indeed devoted his whole life to that problem. He
also, after "ardent effort" to come to terms with the traditional learning, had to cast it aside and turn instead to nature,
observation, and experience. He gave a full account of the
trials and errors along his thorny spiritual path and of the
high exaltation of the sudden moments of illumination. In
the great Book of Nature he did indeed learn the true "course
of the stars," how one planetary "spirit speaks to the other
spirit" in harmonious converse, and how the whole macrocosm of "creative nature" is held together in an intricate
reciprocal exchange of forces,

> "From Heaven through Earth all onward winging,
> Through all the All harmonious ringing."

Kepler was a deeply religious, eminently mystical, and
superbly imaginative man who transmuted many pages of
his scientific works into inspiring poetry. Near the end of
the fifth book ("On the Perfect Harmony of the Planetary
Courses"), he used the sun as the symbol of ultimate truth,
as Goethe did in the opening scene of the second part. Having
defined the excellence of the earth, Kepler goes on to say:
"In the sun, truly (I may imagine) there dwells the direct
intellectual insight, the intellectual fire, the divine intelligence, as the source of every harmony, of whatever kind.
. . . Ah, do not the perceptions cry out together, 'Here dwell

the ardently glowing bodies, capable of comprehending ultimate concepts; and truly the sun is of intellectual fire, if
not king, then at least royal'?"[32] The mystical and symbolical
importance of light in *Faust* and in Goethe's other poetry
has frequently been observed and also connected with his
scientific work, but much background study still remains
to be done.

From such passages we can readily understand why Kepler,
like the earlier Pico, is a good example of the kind of Renaissance personality which the mechanistic rationalists of the
eighteenth century and the prosaic materialists of the nineteenth century simply could not take as he was. Kepler could
not be relegated to oblivion as so many of his like-minded
contemporaries were, for his epoch-making discoveries were
too integral a part of the new science. "The irony of fate
built the mechanical philosophy of the eighteenth century
and the materialistic philosophy of the nineteenth out of the
mystical mathematical theory of the seventeenth. The life and
labors of Kepler protest."[33] Therefore his works were carefully screened, the "acceptable" and "respectable" brought forward with due praise, the rest shoved as far into the background as possible, labeled the aberrations of a great mind or
excused as the accumulated superstition of those times. The
more generous among the materialists did try to be fair-
minded and tolerant toward Kepler. But symptomatic of
different times is Eddington's (and others') acceptance of
Kepler just as he was: "Kepler was guided by a sense of
mathematical form, an aesthetic instinct for the fitness of
things. ... After Kepler came Newton, and gradually mechanism came into predominance again. It is only in the latest
years that we have gone back to something like Kepler's
outlook, so that the music of the spheres is no longer drowned
by the roar of machinery."[34] Which view of the matter Goethe
took, we all know.

Despite these impediments to the understanding of Kepler

in the past, it must be added that the works containing the parallels and analogues to Goethe's *Faust* have long since been readily available, not only in the original Latin but also in German translation: the *Harmonices* in relatively adequate selection—though free translation—since 1918 (completely and well translated in 1939); the *Somnium* since 1898; others since the 1930's.[35] The *Somnium* is one of the great imaginative works of German literature, of towering creative phantasy. Its influence on the English poetic imagination of John Donne, John Milton, John Wilkins, Henry More, and others has been well established in recent research,[36] but not one word about it is to be found in any history of German literature that I have seen. What I offer here in the way of *Faust* analogues from Kepler is a mere suggestive beginning; to give more would upset the balance of this inquiry and yet not be an acceptable substitute for a separate study. With the growing interest in Kepler and a better understanding of his work, this theme will doubtless soon be developed more fully.

CHAPTER VII

THE EASTER WALK AND BEYOND

HE *Pandora* of Benedict Figulus of Hagenau is a remarkable collection of tracts by one of the most fervent of Paracelsians, esteemed during his century even in England and America. We have already noticed one tract contained in it, "The Revelation of the Secret Spirit." More important for us, however, is the second dialogue of Alexander von Suchten and especially the introduction by Figulus himself, which is one of the most characteristic documents of the whole movement. In general outline and some detail these two sections anticipate motifs of the first part of *Faust* and much of the speculative matter contained in the "Easter Walk" scene ("Before the Gates").

In the dialogue, von Suchten tries to explain the deeper meanings of Paracelsus to a baffled neophyte and also the fateful errors not only of the opponents but also of the disciples of Paracelsus who followed the letter rather than the spirit of the master: "But I see that these good gentlemen still adhere to the letter, even as I formerly held it in high esteem." The young practitioners went out and confidently applied their newly learned remedies, but what happened? "The farmers that took them died, became bent and crippled." When the young physician then reported back to his preceptor, the answer was, "You are still a young physician, the practice cannot be learned so quickly, you must get experience in it, kill off and butcher the people briskly, then you will develop into a real physician."

Wagner's extenuating remarks after Faust's bitter self-reproaches,

97

> "Does not a good man do his part
> In practicing transmitted art
> Exactly and with good intent?"

find their parallel in von Suchten's sarcastic account of a group of doctors in consultation on the illness of a young prince: "I was there myself when a young prince was ill and they did not know which way to turn; then one of them spoke, 'Let us proceed according to method and we shall be excused.' How do you like this counsel? Your method must stand, even if all the princes give up the ghost for its sake."

He also alludes to the Paracelsians who interpret their master's work literally and concoct chemical medicines with which they kill off people. Von Suchten's conclusions are:

"The science is above human understanding, a gift and a wondrous work of God; he who proposes to grasp the same with human understanding, he errs. Without revelation of the Holy Spirit and inspiration of God no one will secure it, whether he be Bachelor, Master, or Doctor. Our arts from the universities do not help us in this mystery."

"The letter is a cause of all error, and no one is willing to see that the letter is dead."

"Paracelsus has no greater enemy than the Galenical physicians, they persuade themselves that when they come to a book and read it, they know what it says. But these learned oafs do not reflect that Paracelsus wrote his books in magical terms. Their brain is so full of wit that the magic intellect cannot get in. Therefore they cry, 'Magic is witchcraft, beware, it is the work of the Devil'; whereas magic is not witchcraft at all, but the very greatest wisdom of divine work and a discernment of hidden nature."[1]

The introduction by Figulus begins with a historical survey of the fragmentation and obfuscation of the traditional philosophy, which (in the spirit of Pico) must be brought together again and clarified in an all-embracing synthesizing philosophy. But the point of departure for such a correlation cannot be the acquisition of all book learning, however far-reaching and comprehensive. The learning of the universities can only produce doctrinaire fragments, "disjecta membra," without binding elements or living spirit. The unifying, synthesizing philosophy must be gathered from three books: the book of nature, the Macrocosm; the book of man, the Microcosm; and the book of God, the Bible. Faust's true though unorthodox religiousness, as in the translation scene, later in "Forest and Cavern" and in the "catechizing" scene with Margarete, is integrally related to this whole tradition from Cusanus and Pico onward. Let us follow Figulus' line of thinking up to his reflections on the nature of man where it comes to be of most vital importance for our understanding of Faust. The Paracelsian spirit of it is quite apparent but the expression is succinct and original. The one passage as a whole offers a series of analogies closer to *Faust* than any comparable passage of the master: "If, however, we desire to seek after and learn to know the true natural philosophy established from the light of nature ... where and from whom should we study it? Should we seek the doctors and preceptors of it at the universities? There surely we shall not find it.... They would rather remain with the husks and chaff which the wind scatters hither and thither than with the noble savoury kernel, rye and wheat, out of the great granary or treasury room of the eternal God ... that is, the Macrocosm. ... Where then shall we seek it, in which school, I ask? ... Out of the light of nature ... we should learn. ... Whatever comes from the light of nature, that must be learned from the same ... [Figulus here contrasts the means to a knowledge of earthly things with the means to a knowledge of divine things]. Where then must we come to our intent and the exploration of nature ... ? At home behind the stove we certainly shall not learn it, even though we had the books of all the philosophers together in a heap and stormed around in them day and night, wishing to learn from them. No, that will not do it; on the contrary, if we wish to explore nature in our philosophy and arrive at a desired happy end, we must traverse the books of nature with our feet. Writing we search out through its letters, nature, however, from land to land. . . . Therefore, as often as a land is to be found, so often is a page to be found in the book of nature: thus the codex of nature is sufficiently ample and large. So we have to turn over its pages with our feet and explore them with the spirit of reason. . . . For all creatures and works of God are living letters and books to describe the origin of man: yes, all created things are letters in which we can read who man is. . . .

"Therefore I am justly satisfied with these three books out of which I may draw and learn all wisdom, as [firstly] with the great, mighty, circle-round book of nature which is not written with ink or stylus but with the finger of God. . . . Which book is called Macrocosmus. Secondly, with the small book which with all its leaves and parts is taken from the large one and formed according to it; which book is man . . . and this is called Microcosmus. And it is man alone who is an instrument of the light of nature for its realization, for demonstrating those same works in the arts and in wisdom, as God has ordained them in the firmament. Thus He has also ordained furthermore that man have a twofold magnet [or attractive power]: one, that is, from the elements, therefore he draws these to himself again, the other from the firmament, out of which he draws unto himself the microcosmic sensibilities . . . , and thus the reason of man has a magnet which draws unto itself senses and thoughts from the firmament. . . . Therefore we should also note well that there are two souls in man, the eternal and the natural; that is, two lives, one is subject to death, the other resists death, and thus also two spirits, the eternal and the natural. . . .

"The third book, finally, is the Holy Bible, the sacred revered Scriptures of the Old and New Testament; it guides us into these two aforementioned books. . . ."[2]

The relation of much of this to *Faust* is clear, and indeed only two points require further comment. Let us see first what these excerpts have to offer us toward the understanding of the passage on the two souls, and then proceed to the translation scene. On the first point especially we shall have to go rather far afield to attain proper perspective and to prevent habitual misunderstanding. Again, therefore, a word of caution: the religious and philosophical notion that man has two souls is very ancient and widespread, and it would be possible to cite a variety of examples for this belief—and also a few examples stating that man has three, four, or more souls.[3] Clearly then, an isolated statement from an ancient, medieval, or Renaissance work that man has two souls would not necessarily be of any significance for Goethe's *Faust*; it may not even be a true analogy because the implications of the theory differ widely. The most generally accepted belief is that there is in man a good, heavenly soul in conflict with an evil, earthbound soul. This is indeed so common that the well-known passage in the drama is often interpreted accordingly, though a more appropriate explanation is quite evidently called for.

To indicate the background and chief origins as briefly as possible: Plato in the tenth book of *The Laws* suggested the theory that there are two world souls, a good and an evil soul, and Plutarch, for one, followed him in this, possibly also influenced by the familiar Oriental dualism of the conflict between the good principle and the evil principle. Since every individual soul is a fragment of the world soul, and since man is a compound of the heavenly and earthly, he must have within himself two souls, one heavenward tending and good, the other earthbound and evil. The one is rational, free, and from God; the other animates the body and is subject to the vicissitudes of the sub-lunary world.

This came to be the orthodox and prevalent theory, and at first glance Faust's utterance seems to conform fairly well to it. But on closer scrutiny it becomes clear that Goethe here, as so often in *Faust*, follows heretical, anti-orthodox convictions, and is therefore liable to be thoroughly misunderstood. Goethe, like Figulus, does not state or imply, does not wish to state or imply, that the earthbound, temporal soul is evil, that the conflict is one of good and evil. It is not necessary to impute such an attitude to Goethe, for he is here following an old and excellent precedent of objective, non-moralistic observation of human duality; more than that, it leads to grave misinterpretations of the drama as a whole to impose an orthodox moralism on this passage.

The one soul is naturally "higher" and more "aspiring" than the other, but it would be contrary to Goethe's whole philosophy of life to condemn, suppress, and deny the other soul for that reason. Even in the fifth act when Faust's heavenly soul is ascending and being separated from its earthly increment, the comment of "the more perfected angels" shows not so much a condemnation of the latter (except that it is out of place in the supra-terrestrial regions), as it shows a confirmation of the intimate fusion during life on earth:* "When the strong power of the human spirit has assimilated the elements to itself, then no angel can separate the united dual nature of the two intimately merged; Eternal Love alone can separate it." This process of the separation of the earthly from the heavenly after death is a common accompanying feature of the ascent of the souls in various ancient religions.[4]

What, then, is the more exact source of Goethe's deviation from the good-evil dualism? The answer has already been suggested in the previous chapter. The origins lie in those schools of ancient thought which conceived of the whole of creation as coming from God, and of matter as something divine and therefore good. The early and middle Stoa took over this attitude though the later, more ascetic Stoa (and some individuals earlier) inclined to the conventional dualism. In the centuries around the beginning of the Christian era, in Alexandria, for instance, there were also certain secondary movements which continued the tradition and opposed the prevalent philosophical vilification of the material as against the spiritual and intellectual. This opposition respected the material as a divine and valid part of the world, and considered phenomena not as illusions but as true expressions and manifestations of the spiritual. A necessary corollary is that evil too is forced into the service of God and is made subservient to His ineffable design. "The most exact statement of Stoic doctrine would seem to be that evil exists indeed, but is not the equal of the good either in intensity or in duration; it is an incident, not a first principle of the universe."[5] This is precisely the attitude expressed in the "Prologue in Heaven," when the Lord classes Mephisto among the spirits of negation who perform a useful task in stirring man to activity and who must, ironically, though devils, contribute to the work of creation. Mephisto resentfully admits as much later on in his first colloquy with Faust.

This tradition of the subservience of evil was continued, on the one hand, in Jewish Alexandrian and Cabalistic thought, and came to constitute a marked feature of the *Zohar*. On the other hand, it was perpetuated in the so-called Hermetic writings. The dialogue between Poemander and Hermes contains, as we have seen, a statement of the duality of man, but under the picture of the intimate loving embrace of heaven and earth. Material nature, far from being evil, is "a beautiful image of God." From the Stoic, Hermetic, and Cabalistic writings these convictions were taken over by Cusanus, Pico, Reuchlin, and others, and poured into the main stream of

Renaissance thought—leaving not even Neoplatonism unmodified.

Such a convinced Platonist as Ficino departs radically from ancient Neoplatonism and clearly expresses the opinion that it is man's place and function to stand in a conciliatory middle relation between the earthly and the heavenly, elevating the one by transmitting to it the power of the other: "Wherefore by a natural instinct he ascends to things above and descends to those beneath. And while he ascends he discards not the lower, and while he descends he forsakes not the higher. For if he relinquish either he will lapse to the opposite extreme, neither will he be the true bond of the external world."[6] This double and opposing relation of man can be his tragedy but is intended to be his triumphant glory. He cannot forsake his difficult position and commit himself to either direction without ceasing to be a man, without failing in his creative mediatory calling.

This approval of the world of phenomena and matter was a welcome philosophical confirmation of what was already a firm, vital conviction and a mainspring of action. Most of Renaissance art, even of religious art, was an apotheosis of the material, a glorification of the human body, of fabrics, jewels, and all the accessories of living, of human environment in man-made architecture and God-made landscape. The expansionism of the era, through science and exploration in the realm of space, through historical study and utopianism in the realm of time, represents altogether a positive turning of man toward the material world for the purpose of suffusing it with his own mediatorial spirit, forming and ennobling it, humanizing it, and raising it toward the divine.

We have seen that when a poet such as Tasso or Spenser wanted to express the twofold, magnetic attraction of man heavenward and earthward, he did not make that a conflict between good and evil; when man after his aspiring surge upward comes down to earth again, that is considered something natural and good. In the Renaissance poets, as in Goethe, there is a complete awareness of the tension and conflict and of the human unhappiness that results when the pull in opposite directions is too strong; but this is accepted as the natural lot of man, and there is no thought of an ascetic denial of the earthly and a denunciation of it as primarily evil.

That this approving recognition of the earthly is truly Goethe's attitude can be seen not only from a direct examination of the two-souls passage in its proper setting but also from many another poetic expression and personal statement of his: quite drastically, for instance, in his poem "Great is the Diana of the Ephesians" and in the related letters to and about Jacobi, very beautifully in the last act of *Faust* in the hero's own statement and in Lynceus' hymn of praise to the world of appearances, and in the late poem, "Legacy" ("Vermächtnis"). This salient feature of Goethe's thought is, of course, fully recognized, but its implications for such passages as the one under consideration have at times been neglected.

There is then a long tradition for Goethe's more objective, undogmatic evaluation of the two souls in man, and it is largely a matter of convenience that Figulus specifically has been cited for the Renaissance expression of this idea that there are two souls in man, the eternal and the natural, and with them a twofold attractive power drawing him heavenward and earthward. Nowhere else that I know of does such a statement occur so well phrased to parallel Faust's and in such intimate relation to other "Faustian" motifs. The proper positive attitude toward both attractions is indicated unmistakably in the statement of Ficino.

With the main cause of misunderstanding removed, we can more safely venture to consider another problem in this passage upon which agreement has not yet been reached. There seems to be a difficulty about the one and the other "drive" or "impulse" ("Trieb") in connection with the two souls. Whether or not the mistaken attempt is made to pair off the two drives with the two souls, some confusion seems to remain in most commentaries and some violence is done to the total context.

If we remember, to begin with, that Wagner has just characterized himself specifically as a humanist antiquarian with a special passion for manuscripts, we are on our way toward an explanation which does not have to gloss over or shrug off a single word in the speech of Faust that follows:

> "By one impulse alone are you impressed.
> Oh, never learn to know the other!
> Two souls alas! are dwelling in my breast;
> And each is fain to leave its brother.
> The one, fast clinging, to the world adheres
> With clutching organs, in love's sturdy lust;
> The other strongly lifts itself from dust
> To yonder high, ancestral spheres."[7]

Faust observes that Wagner is conscious of only one drive, namely antiquarian study, which brings him serenity and happiness. He then adjures him not to learn to know the other drive, obviously because it would make him unhappy, as it had Faust. He proceeds to reflect on the kind of unhappiness this other drive has produced within his own self. It has brought about a dangerous tension between his two souls which is tearing him apart between his strong love of earth and his heaven-aspiring urge toward the sphere of the "heroes," the exalted ancestors. At the moment, he sees no way of reconciling the two.

The difference between Faust and Wagner, then, lies in their drives, not in Faust having two souls whereas Wagner presumably has only one. We cannot for a moment infer that Faust arrogates two souls to himself and similar geniuses and implicitly denies that ordinary mortals are so equipped. There is nothing in the long history of this belief that would permit such an interpretation, nor does the text in any way demand it. It is rather that for a man of Faust's kind of drive the two souls pull apart to a high pitch of tension which is perilous and can become tragic if a break results. On the other hand, Wagner's kind of drive does not cause such violent conflict, and the individual active under its impulse is not tragically torn apart but can conveniently satisfy both his modest earthly and his modest spiritual needs.

The drive of Wagner is centripetal, striving toward containment, toward the encompassing and ordering of accumulated knowledge. That makes him the good antiquarian and academician. The drive of Faust is centrifugal, striving toward expansion, the conquest of new realms of knowledge and insight. While the one tends to trim the world down to his size, the other tries to enlarge his capacity to the ever increasing dimensions of his developing understanding.

Wagner's two souls, therefore, become problematic only rarely and mildly. For him learning is an end in itself and a sufficient validation of life. Through his profession he is satisfying his "higher" soul to the limit of his capacity, and also taking good care of the creature comforts of his earthbound soul. He is a typically "well adjusted" individual, self-contained within his limited sphere, with his two souls generally in peaceful agreement. He interprets Faust in his own terms, seeing his powerful aspirations as similar to his own occasional "queer, capricious hours," though admitting that he had never yet felt such a drive.

By contrast, Faust is obsessed by this other drive, the restless expansive one of the speculative mind, of the full-blooded, active genius impelled both by an insatiable lust for life and by an unquenchable thirst for transcendent ultimates. Full self-realization for this type of man in the Renaissance meant the imaginative development and expansion of his individual microcosm to correspond harmoniously to the macrocosm, to include the fullness of all possible human experience, earthly and heavenly. In the "Prologue in Heaven" Mephistopheles sarcastically characterized Faust's expansive drive:

> "He asks of heaven every fairest star
> And of the earth each highest zest,
> And all things near and all things far
> Can not appease his deeply troubled breast."[8]

In contrast to this sneering distortion, the unquenchable impulse is expressed with simple dignity at the moment of Faust's exalted insight on contemplating the sign of the Earth Spirit:

> "I feel the courage, forth into the world to dare;
> The woe of earth, the bliss of earth to bear,"[9]

and even more feelingly in the opening lines of the new additions to the "Fragment" of 1790:

> "Whatever to all mankind is assured,
> I, in my inmost being, will enjoy and know,
> Seize with my soul the highest and most deep;
> Men's weal and woe upon my bosom heap;
> And thus this self of mine to all their selves
> expand. . . ."[10]

It is significant that in the very next lines of both passages Faust consciously faces the possibility that such a course of action may well lead to personal shipwreck. It often did, and the clear awareness of that sinister companion to the fullness of life gave the Renaissance much of its strong sense of tragedy.

With respect to his drive, Faust contrasts with Wagner in his greater capacity, which allows him to sense that there are alluring realms of the spirit beyond the range of the average human understanding and also realms of experience on earth which he has completely neglected during his single-minded search for unattainable ultimates. Here is a magnificent human sphere unfilled and threatening to break apart. Faust has earnestly striven to fill it, but has chosen the wrong method and declares his bankruptcy. His great unrealized capacity is sustained by only one frail body, by only one lifetime, the best part of which he has spent on his purely spiritual and intellectual pursuits which have left him empty and barren (or so he thinks at the moment, not realizing their future value in a truer context).

He has neglected the tangible and attainable of this earth for the intangible and unattainable. Had he pushed this tendency to the extreme he contemplated, with suicide on that critical night, his failure would have been complete, for the very reason that he failed with the Earth Spirit: he was attempting a direct approach without the necessary understanding which the full experience of life on earth would have given him. As he raises the cup to his lips to force the release of his heaven-tending soul from its earthly limitations so that it might soar up to its desired insights, he hears the first bells of Easter morning and the song, "Christ is risen." Christ's greatest triumph comes with his resumption of his fleshly body; he will once more walk with it on earth, and then ascend *with it* to heaven, thus completing his victory over eternal death. With Faust's childhood memories and his deep-seated, intuitive grasp of Christian symbol, he senses that a violent rejection of the earthly will not bring him the desired spiritual freedom. The Word itself was made flesh and dwelt among us. Man cannot fulfill his divine destiny on earth by a denial of the flesh. It is symbolical that Faust refrains from the folly of seeking to leave the material on the festival day of Christ's reunion with the material. He lowers the cup and says in simple, meaningful conclusion, "the earth has me again."

He is given another opportunity for another life, and at first the pendulum swings violently in the other direction toward paying the earthly soul its due and taking into himself the fullness of this world's experiences. With divine irony, however, the course of action and experience on which he embarks in despair and reckless abandon, with drastic, severing words, unexpectedly proves to be the solution of his souls' conflict. He finds the fulfillment of his ideal striving growing naturally out of his earthly achievement. This is quite in harmony with the characteristic Renaissance solution as we have already observed it in the sonnets of Tasso and Spenser, and can observe it in the great artists of the High Renaissance: they willingly recognize the earth as man's normal sphere which he can leave only on rare brief flights, and therefore they creatively shape the earthly to symbolize the heavenly and to rise toward it. Faust at first thinks he has abandoned his transcendent quest but actually he has entered upon the only way to its eventual attainment. His goal has always been the right one and now he is finding the traversable path to it.

That Goethe's intent was exactly that, we can learn not only from the last act where Faust affirms his earthly standpoint and the angels confirm the perfect fusion; we can also learn it from the other set of verses that the poet wrote on the conflict of the two souls: "And what people think is all the same to me. I should like to be at one with myself, however we are 'at two': and in life activity we are a here, a there; the one loves to remain, the other would like to depart. But for coming to self-understanding there is perhaps still a solution: after joyous recognition let the swift deed ensue."[11]

Faust being what he is, life experience can no more become an end in itself than learning had been previously. That is why Mephistopheles can never win, for no stage in Faust's career on earth, no phase of it however entrancing, can have any value in itself. It can only be a means to that great end of accomplishing his destiny as a man on earth. On the highest level of human integration, and after a long, troublous, errant life of assimilating the whole world of space and time which the "exalted ancestors" have left as his human heritage on earth, he ends by finding his two souls united in such harmonious accord of means and ends that they no longer seem like two.

Faust has learned the great human lesson taught by antiquity and again by the Renaissance that man has been given his unique middle position so that he may act as a binding element between the material and the spiritual, infusing the one with the other. Man while he is on earth can find proper employment for his heaven-tending soul only by dedicating it to the shaping, molding process befitting his position. In a humanly restricted way he is given an opportunity to participate in the divine act of creation. It is symbolic that Faust for his last earthly activity chooses to transform one small corner of chaos, confused and fruitless, into a cosmos, ordered and fruitful, which will eventually grow into a free (albeit perilous) land for a free and energetic people.

It is necessary that Faust in the end give expression to the great lesson he has learned, and he did so in words that have frequently been misunderstood because they have not been seen in the context of the whole and from the point of view that prevails throughout the drama. They are the seemingly complete antithesis to his words on that terrible night just before dawn when he was moving toward his great denial of the flesh through suicide. Now in the end he utters his affirmation:

"Well do I know the sphere of earth and men.
The view beyond is barred to mortal ken;
A fool! who thither turns his blinking eyes
And dreams he'll find his like above the skies.
Let him stand fast and look around on earth;
Not mute is this world to a man of worth.
Why need he range through all eternity?
Here he can seize all that he knows to be.
Thus let him wander down his earthly day;

111

When spirits spook, let him pursue his way;
Let him find pain and bliss as on he stride,
He! every moment still unsatisfied."[12]

This declaration cannot properly be interpreted as a denial of transcendent ultimates at the opposite extreme of Faust's early attempt to deny earthly limitations. It is, on the contrary, the sane and realistic appraisal of the only way in which man on earth can develop the fullest potentiality and effectiveness in his given middle position, satisfying the just demands of both souls and bringing them to salutary and fruitful accord. A concentration on another, inaccessible world is not only futile and foolish, it is impious, since it frustrates man's effective self-development in his God-given position, thus negating God's purpose. If Faust's words were godless blasphemy, he could not be saved, for he does not retract them. On the contrary, the implications of the drama are that if man were to deny the earthly soul and soar up toward transcendent ultimates, he would be guilty of a cowardly desertion of the perilous post where he has been placed and where alone he can be effective in this life.

The Lord acknowledges that Faust has done the best that can be expected from frail, fallible man on earth, that he has fulfilled his mission by living up to his capacities, developing himself into a significant microcosm rounded out for perfect harmonious response to the laws of the macrocosm, and exerting his developed powers in a noble act of creativity, redeeming a portion of chaos to ordered, integrated natural life. He thereby becomes a fit subject for divine grace; the Lord considers him ready now, as he was not earlier, to be translated "to other spheres of pure activity"—even as Goethe liked to imagine that the great benign entelechy of Wieland would after death be put to a task befitting the largeness of development it had attained. Wieland, of course, had in his matchlessly graceful way already shown how the two souls in man could be released from their violently separative tension and be brought into a balanced relation which permitted the truer and fuller development of both. Goethe agreed with this solution, though naturally for such a character as Faust (or Michelangelo) more heroic means had to be employed.

To return to the "Easter Walk," Faust at this point, with the strong yearning of his two souls in a twofold direction, is exercising a strong magnetic attraction (Figulus, like Paracelsus, also uses the metaphor "suction," "saugen," as does the Earth Spirit with reference to Faust's strongly attractive yearning). He thus quite naturally in the very next line addresses the aerial spirits through whose spheres he wishes to soar; and quite as naturally a sinister emissary from the earth sphere starts circling around him, in the form of a black poodle. It is an exquisite bit of irony, incidentally, that unintuitive Wagner should fall into an erudite dither at the call to the aerial spirits and then see only commonplace (or even engaging) canine qualities about the poodle. I bring out these connections, not only because they have never been noted, but because the fragmentalists among the commentators have expressed or implied that there is a disturbing break between the two lines,

"To yonder high, ancestral spheres."

and

"Oh, are there spirits hovering near."[13]

There is, on the contrary, through this whole scene a complete, meaningful continuity, which also goes over to the translation scene that immediately follows.

The enigmatic translation scene in *Faust* must be understood in the larger context of what leads up to it both in the drama and in intellectual history. Taking it by itself, and judging its poetic intent from the point of view of a philosophy not pertinent to it, has led many a student to grave misunderstandings or even to a condemnation of the stages by which Faust moves from "In the beginning was the word," to "In the beginning was the act." To understand this scene correctly, we must call to mind two historical phenomena, the first being of decisive importance. Heraclitus had already developed the implications of "Logos" from mere "word" to "meaning," "cosmic law." That is the first stage in Faust's extension also, and his further extensions from "meaning" to "power" to "act" likewise have good precedents in antiquity. The Stoics continued the development of "Logos" to mean the "seed power," the "logos spermatikos," the Divine potentiality of creation, and finally the actor and act of creation. As Cicero reports, Zeno already spoke of the "Logos" or Divine reason as the power which pervades and gives shape to the universe. According to Philo, who is here probably following Posidonius, the "logoi" are the "operative ideas" or "dynameis." "Logos" then is a dynamic, not a static concept. The author of the Gospel was no doubt also aware of the extension, for he goes on to say of the Divine "Logos," "In Him was life," and "All things were made by Him." Professor Faust was not being an irresponsible subjectivist at this point, he was being an excellent classical philologist, solidly traditional and thoroughly grounded in the history of the concept from Heraclitus to St. John.[14] What he was intent upon here was not any specious self-justification for willful inner impulses, but an analysis of the stages of the creative process.

We should also remember, in the second place, that the Gospel of St. John from early times onward held a very special place in the affections of contemplative spirits, and particularly that the beginning of the gospel was used through the Middle Ages, the Renaissance, and beyond, for purposes of white magic, specifically for the exorcism of evil spirits.[15] If we keep in mind the concluding half of the "Easter Walk"

which preceded, we can understand why Faust upon his return to his study, when he felt the impulse toward divine
things and toward translating the Bible into German, should
open the New Testament not to St. Matthew, but to the
fourth Gospel, to St. John. It was the magic, theurgic impulse in him, to try this third way, this "third book," too, as
an approach to the central mysteries; for, as Figulus states,
"it guides us into these two aforementioned books."

Faust's revision of the initial passage, "In the beginning was
the word," went from "word" to "meaning" to "power" to
"act" ("Wort," "Sinn," "Kraft," "Tat"), the transition from
the second to the third especially troubling the commentators. This is not to be interpreted as a reprehensible example
of Faust's subordinating "reason" to "will" and succumbing
to a dangerous "Willensphilosophie." It is to be taken in its
larger context as a simple, natural description of the magical
process, beginning with the "word," which is valid because
it is a symbol for the "meaning" lying behind it (remember
Figulus' description of the book of nature). The comprehension of this "meaning" gives the magus the "power" over
the forces of nature, this "potentiality" in its turn coming to
realization in the "act" (the "deed"). All this was for the
Renaissance philosopher parallel in its minor human way to
God's creation of the world; again remember Figulus' words,
that man is to demonstrate "those same works in the arts and
in wisdom as God has ordained them in the firmament."
God's creation started with the word, within which stood
the whole cosmic meaning, then the whole implicit potentialities of the universe, and finally the explicit act of creation.

In Goethe's prose eulogy, "Third Pilgrimage to Erwin's
Grave in July, 1775," we can also observe that his concept
of the artistic process goes from the "idea of creation," to the
"power of creation," to the "work of creation." The analogy
to divine creation is even more clearly stated in the contem-
poraneous "Falkonet" essay.[16] Like so much else, this analogy

too can be traced back to Cusanus, where the implications are quite like those underlying the third section of Faust's resumed monologue after Wagner leaves him.[17]

Faust's progression then, from word to act is to be understood as a sequence of ever deeper penetration, not as an antithesis, not as a denial of the word. As Cassirer paraphrases Pico: "The word of the Bible is indeed the highest; but it speaks only to him who cracks the hard shell of the *mere* word. Within this hard shell of the Divine law as written there lies the Divine meaning: the *'sensus anagogicus,'* which alone leads truly upward, and not only procures for us entrance to the world of spirits, but also solves its deepest secrets."[18]

Or as Cassirer outlines the implications of the movement initiated by Cusanus:

"The process of secularization is completed when the revelation of the Book of Nature is set up alongside the revelation of the Bible. No fundamental contradiction can exist between the two, since both present the same spiritual meaning in variant form, since in them the oneness of the divine originator of nature is manifested. If nevertheless, according to appearances, such a conflict opens up before us, then the resolution can only ensue in this manner, that we give preference to revelation in the work before that in the word; for the word comes from the past and is handed down to us, whereas the work stands before us as something present and lasting, something that can be examined directly here and now."[19]

CHAPTER VIII

CUSANUS AND THE UNITY OF *FAUST*

S A LAST PARALLEL, there is a set of concepts which are as all-pervasive and intricately interrelated in *Faust* as they are in their originator, Nicolaus Cusanus, or in his disciple Pico. This threefold set of concepts (to be thought of as being in intimate and reciprocal interrelation) is the principle of learned ignorance (the knowledge of not knowing), the principle of the coincidence (the union) of opposites, and the symbolic knowledge of God. Just as Pico's philosophy until a very few years ago was conceived of as an eclectic hodge-podge of disparate and irreconcilable elements collected together from all ages and all regions, and thus no philosophy at all,[1] just so, despite valiant and largely successful attempts to prove the contrary, has *Faust* been conceived of as Goethe's happy dumping ground for all kinds of ideas and opinions of his, and even for pieces that were originally intended for another purpose. On the surface a disjointedness is at times apparent and even obtrusive, though it is not at all as far reaching as one might at first believe. Below this surface appearance, from the point of view of Pico's philosophical intent and of Goethe's poetic intent, the claim that *Faust* contains many a fortuitous accretion is not true at all, but rests on a misunderstanding of the work.

Cusanus, and Pico after him, begin with the ancient insight that mortal man cannot know ultimate truth, cannot look at God, at the source of light, face to face. This concept leads them to the corollary that man can and must see God, the truth, in all the ways and forms in which He manifests Himself to man. Each of these manifestations tells us one thing or another about the ultimate source—the drawback is,

117

however, that for our human understanding, which cannot see the whole pattern, these manifestations tells us very different, paradoxical, and often downright contradictory things.

In the mind of God all these seeming contradictions fuse in a harmonious unity; there is a coincidence of opposites. Thus all phenomena, all philosophical tenets, all theological beliefs are partial, incomplete, earthly metaphors or symbols of an inexpressible and incomprehensible ultimate truth. Our knowledge of God can come to us only through various fragmentary metaphors, can only be a symbolic knowledge of God. On the other hand, each of these symbols or metaphors has a ray of the divine in it and, mutually contradictory though they may be, they all come together in a higher harmony, in a coincidence of opposites.[2]

That, approximately and briefly, is the meaning of Cusanus' three principles of learned ignorance, coincidence of opposites, and symbolic knowledge. Using these three as his philosophical basis, Pico attempted the noble feat of making his age the conciliatory meeting ground of all that the mind of man in all ages and places had tried to conceive, each concept yielding one refracted ray, one partial image of the ultimate truth, and all together giving us a far truer picture of the boundless multiplicity and glorious variety that goes into making up the ultimate truth than any attempt at a flawlessly integrated system possibly could. In the late Renaissance and in the Baroque this tendency and this conviction culminated in the Pansophic movement in Germany; transmitted by Theodore Haak, Samuel Hartlib, and their associates, it made its permanent impress on English (and American) intellectual life.

The failures and shortcomings of man's comprehension are, therefore, not a cause for despair and rebellion. Realization of limitations is simply the first, preliminary position a man must take before he can set out on the quest for the only kind of knowledge which is within the scope of his comprehension: symbolic knowledge, with the reward that he can constantly enrich it with every new insight and human experience, and bring it to a closer approximation to the divine.

Faust has at the beginning of the drama arrived at the preliminary position, misunderstands it as being the end rather than the beginning, and is turned back in his attempt to reach ultimates by means of sheer force of will and desire without adequate preparation. Then, however, he is helped forward in his plunge into the fullness of life, with its heavy accompanying portion of evil and tragedy. His deepening insights both into the approaches to truth and into the larger contexts of meaning, with all their paradoxical juxtaposition of good and evil, can be observed in "Forest and Cavern."[3] In the "catechizing" scene, almost immediately thereafter, Margarete asks Faust about his religion. His eloquent answer, stressing the importance of the belief in God and its universality, and the unimportance and limitation of the outward forms and expressions of this belief—all this is in complete accord with the convictions of Pico (and the even more daring opinions of Pulci), that religious feeling is the important thing, that any belief or doctrine or ceremony (even the Christian) is transitory symbol (though it is truly to be venerated as a significant symbol). Pulci actually asserted that the pagan worshiper of idols, who knew no better and who was truly devout in his religious practices, would be saved.[4] Here again Cusanus showed the way with his great treatise on universal religious tolerance, *De Pace Fidei*.

By the beginning of the second part Faust has at length reached the point of wisdom of Cusanus and Pico, where he can draw the proper conclusions of his not-knowing. He turns his back on the sun, on the quest for ultimates, no longer in rebellious frustration or in impotent yearning, but now in calm realization both of his human limitations and of the rich possibilities the world offers in compensation. (The factor of resignation here should not be overstressed; Faust gains as well as loses.) The ultimate, pure, unendurable light is broken up into the manifold lovely colors and ever shifting form of the rainbow over the waterfall:

"The rainbow mirrors human aims and action.
Think, and more clearly wilt thou grasp it, seeing
We have our life in many-hued reflection."[5]

Faust is willing and ready now to take symbolic knowledge instead of ultimate knowledge, to let all the multifarious strands of life weave together, knowing that they are forming a pattern, though not knowing exactly what that pattern will be, knowing that it is his human duty to take up all the strands he can, to strive toward realizing the most copious constructive design of which his mind is capable.

Philipp Melanchthon, with his profound, lucid, and serene mind, saw this and expressed it well: "The knowledge of many things assured and useful for life is not to be cast aside because of this [incertitude], even though we are ignorant of so much. For truly we know that it is the will of God that we examine his footsteps in the creation of the world and choose things useful for the preservation of life. We are also to prepare ourselves for that eternal academy in which we shall apprehend the entirety of natural philosophy when the Architect Himself will show us the idea [the original plan] of the world."[6]

Goethe himself near the end of his life told Eckermann that the key to Faust's salvation lay in the lines sung by the angels soaring upward with Faust's immortal part:

" 'Who e'er aspiring, struggles on,
For him there is salvation.'

". . . in Faust himself an ever higher and purer activity till the end, and from on high Eternal Love coming to his aid."[7]
When there is an energetic pursuit of insight and experience, undaunted by the fact that on earth its close companions are failure and error, then the divine grace will in the end re-

ward the questing activist with perfect understanding. The reward of the quietist Goethe takes up elsewhere; in *Faust* the ideal of passive abnegation is not pertinent.

It should be noted that Goethe voiced his approval of the Faustian way just after he had discussed with Eckermann the last deep shadow that old Faust had cast upon his world through his incurable restlessness and discontent. Goethe's honesty about the realities of life as it is lived on this earth, in the symbolic Philemon and Baucis episode, has always been a stone of offense to the uncritical admirers of Faust, and a stimulus to folly for his self-righteous and indignant calumniators, both sides taking off from false idealistic premises. We must always take care to follow Goethe's example of interpreting the parts in the spirit of the whole. If this is difficult at times, even seemingly impossible, we should not be indignant and resentful any more than we should be if nature failed to conform to some preconceived notion and neat plan of ours. Seeming disparities only indicate that the design is grander than we are at the moment prepared to comprehend.

The concluding passage of the whole drama, sung by the "Chorus mysticus" in heaven, gives final poetic expression to the threefold condition of human striving on earth, a striving which is not damned for its imperfection and failure but, on the contrary, is the prerequisite for the grace of ultimate insight which is to be bestowed in the world to come:

> "All that is transient
> Is symbol mere;
> The once deficient
> Is realized here;
> The indescribable
> Here it is done:
> The Eternal-Womanly
> Draweth us on."[8]

All that we know in life is but a symbol, a metaphor of the ultimate truth, an inadequate representation of what we shall experience in its entirety, when that which is indescribable on earth (is only suggestible) will be realized and enacted within us. What draws us upward is that which is prefigured here below by the symbol of the womanly, by the great metaphor of the feminine principle in religion: the process of regeneration, of rebirth through love. Thereby finally the upward-drawing, magnetic powers are reinforced by divine grace, raise man beyond the orbit of the downward-drawing powers, and carry him into the higher spheres.

By great good fortune we have Goethe's own statement to indicate that he conceived of *Faust* in something like the many-faceted manner of Cusanus, rather than in the manner of the abstract systematic philosophers of his own day; that he saw Faust's redemption as Pico would have seen it; and that he continued to envision his own poetic creative processes as a harmonious interaction of macrocosm and microcosm, object and subject. We can, therefore, fittingly conclude the chapter with Goethe's fullest statement on his point of view, particularly calling attention to the last sentence where the incommensurableness of the poet's creation is deemed desirable, possibly (we may add) because it thereby comes into closer approximation to the incommensurableness of God's creation, as Cusanus conceived it. Needless to say for those who know Goethe's works, this sentence is not intended to offer precedent or solace for the cultists of pseudo-profundity and unintelligibility. The old poet is speaking to Eckermann in the spring of 1827, making fun, as he so often did, of the abstractionist approach to literature:

"The Germans, by the way, are odd people. By their deep thoughts and ideas, which they seek in everything and impute to everything, they make life more burdensome than need be. Come now, do have the courage, for a change, to give yourself up to impressions, allow yourself to be amused, moved, elated, yes even instructed, inspired and encouraged to something great. But do not forever think that all is vanity if it is not somehow abstract thought and idea.

"Here they come and ask, what idea I meant to embody in my *Faust*. As though I knew that myself and could express it! 'From heaven through the world to hell,' that would do in a pinch; but this is no idea, only the course of action. And further, that the devil loses the wager and that a man always striving upward out of deep error toward something better is to be redeemed—that is, to be sure, an effective, clarifying, good thought, but it is no idea which lies at the basis of the whole and of each individual scene taken separately. It would have been a fine thing indeed if I had strung so rich, colorful, and highly diversified a life as I have brought to view in *Faust*, upon the slender thread of a single pervading idea.

"Altogether, it was not in my nature as a poet to strive to embody something abstract. I received impressions in my mind, impressions indeed of a sensuous, animated, lovely, colorful, hundredfold kind, as an active imagination offered them to me. As a poet I had nothing more to do than round out and develop such views and impressions artistically in myself, and by means of a lively representation so to bring them to view that others might receive the same impressions on hearing or reading my exposition of them."

He goes on to mention some short reflective poems of his, and the one large work, the *Elective Affinities*, which is based on an all-pervading idea and is thus more easily accessible to reason, continuing: "... but I will not say that it was improved thereby. On the contrary, I am of the opinion: the more incommensurable a poetic production is and the more incomprehensible to reason, the better."[9]

CHAPTER IX

CONCLUDING OBSERVATIONS

T WOULD BE POSSIBLE to multiply the connections of *Faust* to the Renaissance many times over, but it is not necessary. The chief question posed by this study is whether the values and principles, the personalities and actions of the drama, in their larger interrelations and sequences, resemble those of the Renaissance more than they do those of Goethe's own age. The answer seems to be, yes, they do. The drama is not subjective and not of the eighteenth century with some decorative Renaissance coloring; it is largely objective, of the Renaissance with some intentional anachronisms and with the personal coloring and blending which accompanied the act of poetic creation. Viewed in its own proper time in which the poet placed it, its seeming discontinuities and contradictions resolve of themselves, and the total work exhibits lines of unity previously unobserved. In its own intellectual atmosphere it lives and breathes, has dimensionality and resonance and coherence. By contrast, it seems to be out of its element in the eighteenth century, for Goethe took into his *Faust* phases of Renaissance conviction and imagination with which his own epoch for the most part was not concerned.

In this particular work Goethe was, in the fullness of his creative originality, an "old-fashioned" artist who clung to the old exalted values of the Renaissance and of a freshly revived antiquity, rejecting the prevailing standards of the Enlightenment, Revolution, and romanticism, as well as the basic assumptions of the philosophies of his day. In technique, too, the protean variety of German, Italian, and Neo-Latin forms in the poem points intentionally and meaningfully to the past (and to the future), as does the vast dramaturgy of

124

Renaissance and Baroque spectacle contrasting with scenes of sensitive intimacy, as does also the unchecked creative boldness of its language which is unparalleled since the days of Shakespeare. That Goethe himself thought of his language and expression as Renaissance in character is indicated by his suggested improvement of the French translations that continued to appear during his old age: Soret reported that Goethe thought *Faust* should be translated into the French of the time of Marot; that means, into Renaissance French, before the drastic pruning of the language. Two years later he repeated the same thought to Cousin. This too, like so much in old Goethe, points back unmistakably to mental associations he had formed in his youth, as a passage in his autobiography tells us: "When in my youthful years my attention was more and more directed to the German quality of the sixteenth century, I soon extended my inclination also to the French of that glorious epoch. Montaigne, Amyot, Rabelais, Marot were my friends and aroused my sympathy and admiration."[1]

For such a long time has the intellectual atmosphere of the eighteenth century, particularly of the Storm and Stress, been studied and taken for granted as the natural environment of the Goethean Faust, that the suggestion of another possibility may be a bit disconcerting. However, the new evidences and demonstrated hypotheses are not necessarily in direct opposition to traditional attitudes, for there are many points of agreement, and both will have to be kept in mind.

Anyone who wishes to estimate the relative scope of the old and the new hypotheses, can make a fairly crucial test if he asks himself the following two questions: What eighteenth-century work aside from Goethe's *Faust* is comparable to Pico's, for instance, for giving an all-over, *structural* outline of the character, place, and destiny of the "Faustian" man? (The factor of structure is decisive and, of course, precludes any anthology of scattered parallels in word and thought, however compendious, and also any incidental or peripheral phases of the work.) Secondly, what actual personalities of the eighteenth century have as many centrally "Faustian" traits about them as have, for instance, Leonardo, Michelangelo, Paracelsus, Dee, Bruno, or Kepler? In answer, Herder's name is almost certain to come up, but not if the characterizations of Herder by Goethe himself, by other contemporaries, and by the modern biographers are kept in mind. The reader may also find it surprising as well as amusing to read what Herder himself had to say about Goethe's *Faust*.

However, the drama goes beyond either Goethe's or Faust's proper period. There is in it from the beginning a tendency toward breaking the temporal shackles; with the sundering of them the action extends backward and forward to conquer all the time of which man's mind is the master. And this again is characteristic of the Renaissance: the three faces of time are virtually a symbol of the fifteenth and sixteenth centuries. Though in a larger sense *Faust* is a timeless drama, as far beyond the limitations of its own period setting as it is beyond Goethe's age or our own, it can properly be called a drama of the Renaissance because that epoch is its point of departure and furnishes its fundamental premises, from which alone its problem, action, and solution can be truly understood. It is naturally not a historical drama, nor does it exhibit any of the traits of that genre except for a few minor details.

The protagonist is a Renaissance man not so much in the sense that he is a specific or a representative personage of that era as in the sense that he stands as the most vital and eloquent symbol of its distinctive and central drive: the will to all-inclusive synthesis—not the medieval synthesis of the *Summa* which subsumes everything to a pre-formed system and method, but a synthesis which allows everything to come together freely, find its own level and natural integration, and gradually emerge out of a seeming confusion into a living, dynamic interrelation of forces and influences. This has a far greater claim to agreement with truth and reality than has the violent procrusteanism of any philosophic system.

Perhaps one of the chief causes of misunderstanding is the tendency to consider *Faust* as a philosophic poem rather than as a symbolic poem. It is a philosophic poem only in the original sense of the word philosophy: love of wisdom. In the stricter sense, however, philosophy distinguishes and divides, symbol identifies and unites. The application of conventional philosophic methods to the criticism of the work has led to some strange misapprehensions, and has sometimes mantled it in deepest obscurity. *Faust* is poetry, *Faust* is symbol, and the poetic symbolic approach can be the only primary one. Though Goethe went to great effort to come to a sympathetic understanding of the systematic and idealistic philosophers of his own day, their way of thought was alien to his own and their way of expression distasteful. Those concepts which he ostensibly took from them, on closer inspection usually turn out to be reformulations of thoughts which he already knew from the older authors he loved. His natural affinities were always for the unsystematic philosophers and especially for those thinkers who believed that all phenomena are symbols, that is, genuine realities in full harmonious relation to the greater and deeper realities which they reveal and conceal.

From the time of Luden's long conversation with Goethe on *Faust*, in 1806,[2] to the present, there have been fervent admirers of the work who have given up the hope of finding the unity within it and have resigned themselves to enjoying its separate beauties and fragmentary greatnesses. There have been others in recent times who have attempted to give a specious unity to it by forcing it into the patterns of their latest philosophical fads, not infrequently doing violence thereby to the express poetic intention of the author. Perhaps they have been led to this subjective and willful course because the philosophies of Goethe's own day cannot be brought into any significant over-all correspondence to the work.

Not nearly as reprehensible as the willfully subjective, often negativistic perversion of the meaning of *Faust*, and yet grave, is the long-standing, particularistic tendency toward seeing Faust the man as a specifically German phenomenon. On the contrary, Faust is throughout and in essentials a European, and only at times and in accidentals a German, even as he is in essentials a Renaissance man, the master of three thousand years, and only in that larger sense a projection of Goethe and his age.

Even as the Germans have often blinded themselves to the wider significance of *Faust*, they have generally concealed from themselves the share they had in the development of the European Renaissance, and have even in extreme cases assumed the attitude of condemning the Renaissance as an evil fate imposed upon them from without which impeded their own organic growth. Such an attitude is incomprehensible to the foreign student who in the course of his special studies has had occasion to observe the enormous prestige which the works of the German spirit enjoyed throughout Europe during the sixteenth and seventeenth centuries, who has noted how many books by Germans were reprinted throughout Europe from Italy to England, and how well stocked with German books were many of the important European and early American libraries.[3] It is just these books of international scope and prestige which have been all too often neglected by the German intellectual historians, who still concentrate upon the exclusively German works that never crossed the frontiers, or upon the works that are imitations of foreign models. Only when they add thereto those works which were admired and imitated abroad, will they really know what the German Renaissance was and how European it was. That is why every larger study of German

Renaissance or Baroque literature thus far has failed of achieving true survey and synthesis.

We may regard it as a symbol that at the very portals of the European Renaissance proper stands a German cardinal, Nicolaus Cusanus, who was not thought of particularly as a German, who was indeed the intimate friend of the first truly 'Renaissance pope, Aeneas Silvius Piccolomini, who moreover in his far-ranging travels and studies made himself the master of Mediterranean civilization, who gave one of the decisive impulses toward the development of the Italian, the German, the European Renaissance, and who in the end in affectionate memory left the volumes that bear witness to his universality to the small town on the Moselle where he was born. Wittingly or unwittingly, directly or indirectly, Goethe was the true heir of Cusanus, and used the framework of his philosophy as the uniting principle for his great work, from Faust's first words to the last words about him.

Nothing which has been said about the work and its author, however, should be construed as implying that Goethe's ways of thinking, feeling, reacting, creating were exclusively or even primarily those of the Renaissance. Though he felt at home in that period, he did not confine himself to its fundamental premises, underlying attitude and outlook, nor did he advocate that they be restored to primacy for his own times or for the future. We know that he wrote not only the masterpiece which was based on these premises but that he also, for example, had the breadth and flexibility of genius to write another masterpiece, a contemporary one, out of his own times and for his own times, namely his *Wilhelm Meister*.

Though a contemporary novel is on a different artistic plane from a symbolic representative drama, and cannot in certain ultimates be compared with it, we can, nevertheless, observe that *Wilhelm Meister* is also in two parts, was begun in youth and finished in old age, that it also breaks through the limits of its own time into a great panoramic vista of the future, and likewise rises above its art form to a higher literary level. But how different are its basic assumptions, its accepted standards and points of view!

Omitting here, of necessity, all discussion of its many resemblances to *Faust*, from the obvious to the very subtle ones, omitting also the discussion of its startlingly advanced exploration of the subconscious and the other X-factors of human existence, let us, for the sake of comparison, state briefly what standards and criteria are assumed and accepted for the life and development of Wilhelm and his associates.

The characters in the novel are thoroughly "modern" people of the period around 1800. They only rarely step out of the framework of reference of their times; the problems they find in their environment and in themselves, the measures they take to solve them are in true correspondence to the age in which they live, move, and have their being.

Wilhelm is the social personality of his day who is educated in society and for society. He quickly acquires the widest possible variety of social relations; all the things he most wishes to do have to be done in cooperation with others; and every significant new stage in his career represents an advance in human understanding and social insight, until we finally see him and his associates developing even beyond their enlightened social-minded aristocracy to the initiation of a great experiment in industrial democracy on American soil, with themselves as equals among other workers—this a vision (or better, an insight) of Goethe's to which no other eminent man of letters was to attain for some time to come.

The complex of basic assumptions and motivations then is something like this: being a useful member of society is the highest ideal; achieving some work which receives social recognition is the highest glory; helping to reform or to establish a society in which a harmonious mutual adjustment is possible, in a carefully balanced reciprocity between the individual and the group, that is the ultimate exalted effort in which a human being can engage. These are, of course, simply the accepted standards and attitudes of the novel, not its ideological framework, theme, or anything of the kind; the work has far greater dimensions.

If we measure *Faust* against these criteria, we can observe an almost total discrepancy. Only the ending is in essential harmony, when old Faust is prepared to lay down his aristocratic rule, since his new land has by that time developed to the point where it can be taken over and maintained by "a free people on a free soil," of whom he would like to be one. There is then an entirely different way, from very different assumptions, toward much the same end.

This similarity of final vision and achievement, together with what God plainly says about Faust in the "Prologue" and what the angelic messengers say after his death, shows us that Goethe emphatically approved of Faust's way through life; his many other statements, in letters and conversations, especially to Eckermann, exclude the possibility of any other interpretation. Since, therefore, the record is completely clear that Goethe commended the life, purpose, and achievement of both Faust and Wilhelm Meister, and since the one will not conform to the basic criteria of the other, we are obliged to ask the question: what are the fundamental premises according to which the life and destiny of Faust are intelligible? The preceding chapters contain the various parts of the answer, but it may be well to summarize it here from another point of view.

To speak in Renaissance symbolic language: man occupies a middle position in the cosmos, comprising within himself the whole range of creation from mass and matter, through plant life and animal sensation, on to the highest cognizance of spirit and intellect, aspiring even toward communion with the Godhead. He thus has an advantage even over the angels:

he is the only one of God's creatures who is able to comprehend within himself, in epitome, the totality of creation.

Man in his unique middle position contains in abstract all the parts and forces of the whole of creation; he even has a due portion of that primordial chaos out of which cosmos and light were born through the seed-power of the divine Logos. He thus owns potentially everything necessary for making himself into a microcosm which can be brought to ever more perfect harmonic correspondence to the macrocosm. Man, with his free choice, can, of course, also sink down to any level on the way toward disintegrated chaos; he can also stop far short of perfection on the way up and attain to only fragmentary correlation and incomplete harmony.

Within the framework of this philosophy the chief duty of man is to develop himself into as full and perfect a microcosm as his natural endowments and powers will permit. Far from being the egoistic aim it may at first seem to be, it is in its Renaissance cosmic setting the most noble and godly action that man can undertake. The doctrine of harmonic correspondence between microcosm and macrocosm implies clearly that man can be effective in this world only to the extent that he has brought himself into harmony with the world, only to the extent that he makes the laws of the universe the principles of his own action. This is old Stoic doctrine, which was developed by Kepler and others, was borrowed by Kant as well as by Goethe, and naturally makes allowance for human imperfection and shortcomings.

Only like can truly know like and be effective in it; thus the more perfect a cosmic replica man can make of himself, the greater will be his understanding of the universe, and the abler will he be to perform the task befitting his middle position between the spiritual and the material. That task is to aid creation on its way upward to God, to spiritualize the material, to give higher integration to lower forms, even to convert a portion of chaos into ordered cosmos. In other words, the Renaissance believed that God intended man to participate in the creative process, on the human level; to the extent that man did so, he was fulfilling his highest destiny and aiding in the elevation and redemption of the world. The history of the word "creation" as applied to human achievement is an indication of the strength and spread of this heterodox conviction.

In the Renaissance the emphasis was on the *individual in* society rather than on the *member of* society. Not that the social obligations of man were repudiated, but that they were assumed to be dependent on even higher obligations. If man fulfilled his divine destiny, the result would be an improvement of the world, and that would include his fellow men. For man to make human betterment his sole purpose would be a reprehensible limitation of his duties which are equally owing to the rest of creation and to God. Social improvement, therefore, cannot be the purpose, but it will be one end result of the right human effort of a good man who has performed for God his ennobling duty toward himself and the world.

It is thus Faust's duty to expand his understanding by the full range of experiences attainable to man, and not to desist from his studies in the great university of the world until he has such a practical and well-rounded comprehension of the laws of life and the cosmos that he feels a spontaneous inner urge to participate in the act of creation on its own terms. (This basis for action is quite unlike the theoretical constructionism of an idealist visionary, whose efforts to foist his artificial social pattern on human reality can lead only to the misery and degradation of mankind.) Faust's last great work is the rescue of one disintegrated, formless, fruitless corner of chaos, turning it into an integrated, formed, fruitful realm of cosmos. Significantly, he concentrated on the work itself, with creative activity his primary purpose, and only near the conclusion did he realize what a glorious future result would come from his microcosmic effort. His previous wanderings through space and time and his stations along the way are, from the Renaissance view, not at all the rootless, purposeless drifting of a self-indulgent tourist, they are the creative, productive fulfillment of his human destiny and God's purpose.

In the "Prologue" the Lord had announced what He expected of Faust; His norms, be it noted, are not social, but far greater and more encompassing. Faust fulfills his mission in the only way a mortal can fulfill such an overwhelming mission. After him man will have higher potentialities, he will have greater strength and confidence to penetrate ever deeper into chaos, to separate and mold it into cosmos, to integrate it into ever higher forms. One end-product or even by-product of a great and good man having lived, searched, and created in this world is that the boundaries of light and vision are thereby extended for the rest of humanity, even if human betterment was not a prime motive force within him.

The Greeks would have called him a "hero" and established him like Heracles or Asclepius among that group of demi-gods, or translated him to a star (a poetic idea of which Goethe was fond). The Renaissance would have granted him unreserved honor with full ceremonial accompaniment, and even recorded his errors and falls with awed respect and the properly humble "how much the more to me."

Goethe decided in conclusion to stage for Faust a full-scale celestial apotheosis, or rather ascension, in an appropriate Renaissance-Baroque manner. Since he thereby indicated that Faust's course on earth had been achieved in accordance with God's will, it might be a bit presumptuous for anyone to lay claim to a judgment better informed than Goethe's and a justice more wisely administered than God's. The poet wanted to give us this other view of life, he felt we needed it, and by this time, looking back over the total results of a century of socially oriented endeavor, we should know whether we do need it and how much we need it.

It is evident from *Wilhelm Meister* that Goethe was not a reactionary who turned back to Renaissance ways and attitudes in denial of his own age and its tendencies. And yet, with astonishing prevision he saw the other side of the developing new century, saw that even its laudable social ideals might suffer the baneful results of their one-sidedness and insufficiency. The conversations with Eckermann are full of this, and there is also the famous letter to Zelter of June 6, 1825, with his devastating prognosis of the nineteenth century.[4]

With unerring intuition Goethe saw that the new age needed what it had already thoughtlessly pushed aside. And so he felt impelled again and again throughout his life to take up a work begun in early youth, even though in his maturity, when the new attitudes predominated in him, he experienced considerable difficulty in recovering once more a conscious understanding of the basic Renaissance assumptions on which he had planned and begun it. By old age he was not only completely clear about it again, he saw it with far wider and deeper perspective. He discerned the threads which ran to it from remotest time, and helped spin the threads which reach from it to his own time and into the future.

To offset the ideal of the skilled and competent specialist perfectly integrated into the social pattern of his day, and withal a fine well-rounded human being, Goethe realized that the world needed the vision of the man who makes it his primary life work to encompass the totality of human experience and insight, to transcend all the barriers of space and time that hem him in as an individual, who perhaps even neglects the demands that his fellow men feel they may reasonably make of him, in order to progress to that great creative synthesizing act which will raise his world to a higher level of integration, and mankind to a higher level of understanding. The world needs such men for its own salvation, since the end product of perfect social integration

135

is complacency, intolerance, stagnation, and a stultifying mediocrity.

Perhaps Goethe never consciously considered just why *Faust* and *Wilhelm Meister*, these two so very different works, should become the occupation of a lifetime. Obviously both were deeply important to him; he had two very different attitudes toward life which he felt it important to express. But we must not forget that he devoted much more attention and loving care to *Faust* than he did to *Wilhelm Meister*, he began it sooner, stayed with it longer, spoke of it more often and more warmly, and left the second part sealed as his last literary testament to the future. The contemporary novel was important to him, but the symbolic representative drama was more important.

Two equally wrong claims can be made, and have been made concerning *Faust*: one, that it is a sure and sufficient guide for modern man; two, that it has nothing to offer our times except a warning example against everything "Faustian." The drama is a poetic masterpiece, not an ethical-philosophical treatise. We should turn to it not to learn precepts for life but to learn life. And life is in it in symbolic, truthful statement, life in all its achievement, in all its frustration, in all its glory, in all its grimness, not as the idealist poet would like it to be, but as the objective poet knows it is. The Philemon and Baucis episode, for example, ought not to have happened, but in the reality for which it is a symbol, it always has happened, in every colonial project in the history of man, even in the most humane and enlightened. It is the poet's duty neither to suppress that side of reality nor to excuse it but only to present it in valid symbol.

In the midst of the world as it is, the poet placed the man with the unquenchable expansive drive, the restless urge to explore all the world's values in every direction, who dared to venture beyond the limits set to mortal man and to bring back with him from beyond what he needed and desired for this life. Like the several Renaissance men we have observed, he mastered the world creatively before he was able to master himself. Through his own fault as well as through the treachery of circumstances he repeatedly fell into error and sin, yet for all that, he developed into a personality of all-encompassing, overwhelming greatness, according to the potentialities with which the poet had endowed him.

Far from being a subjective writer who used the large framework of *Faust* for a vast series of greatly varied and highly colorful personal portraits and scenes in masquerade, Goethe was in the unrolling of this drama the creator of an integrated work, of a full and self-sufficient entity. A true creator must be like God, evolving a vast and complex universe, remaining warm and sympathetic, it is true, but aloof and divinely impersonal, not concealing the faults of his hero, not ameliorating or artificially diverting the terror, the tragedy, and the guilt, allowing the hilarious, the witty, the trivial to enter, as in life, sometimes at incongruous moments, all in the interest of a higher truth than mere surface consistency, letting his figures and events run their own course according to their own bents and conflicts, in brief, giving his creation its own proper life in its own atmosphere.

What may always remain something of a mystery is Goethe's uncanny ability to penetrate to the vital center of the Renaissance. Perhaps with his poetic intuition Goethe created with a deeper truth and accuracy than he knew; perhaps with his great empathic powers delicately controlling the sum of his knowledge, he could view and represent the age of Faust more authentically than any one for the next century and longer. Whatever the case may be, the picture of the Renaissance that has developed out of the far-ranging studies of recent decades corresponds in a remarkable way to the great lines and masses as well as to the details on the canvas of the master.

NOTES

I. THE BACKGROUND

1. In order to determine the consensus of critical opinion on Goethe's *Faust*, both for the general approach and for the solutions of special problems, six of the more modern general commentaries and critical works were regularly consulted, namely those of Robert Petsch (1926), F. Melian Stawell and G. Lowes Dickinson (1928), Eugen Kühnemann (1930, in his *Goethe*), Heinrich Rickert (1932), Georg Witkowski (1936), Reinhard Buchwald (1942). The commentary of Ernst Beutler (1948) was unfortunately, through a mishap in ordering, not available until after the completion of this study. These seven may be taken as representing the present state of *Faust* scholarship, as including that which has commonly been accepted from preceding general and special studies, and as superseding the older general commentaries. A few works that I should like to have consulted were not available to me, others which became available too late for full consideration are represented only in the notes. Many that I did consult, large and small, some of great merit, had no relevancy to the present study beyond what the above mentioned general works contain; though they go undesignated here, they served to assure me that my choice was representative. The more special studies used are noted in their proper places; often they too are cited simply as examples for which others not cited would have served. This by no means excludes the possibility that in the vast sea of *Faust* literature I may have missed one or the other work of special importance for this study, though in that case it has been generally overlooked. My failure, however, to mention such special studies as that on the relation of Johann Valentin Andreae's *Turbo* to *Faust* means not that I am unaware of them but that they are not closely connected with the specific topics taken up in this study. References to works of Goethe other than *Faust* are to the Weimar edition (*W.A.*, Roman division number, Arabic volume number, Arabic page number), though the normalized spelling and punctuation of the Propyläen edition has been adopted.

2. "German Thought and Literature in New England, 1620-1820," *The Journal of English and Germanic Philology*, XLI (1942), 1-45, esp. 6-12; "Unexplored Phases of German Influence on Seventeenth-Century English Literature," paper read at the Germanic Section meeting of the Modern Language Association, December 1946. The writer's forthcoming monograph, *John Winthrop*

the Younger and the World of Learning, will contain a catalogue of the Winthrop family library. For Winthrop's European connections see especially G. H. Turnbull's very important new book, *Hartlib, Dury and Comenius*, University Press of Liverpool, 1947.

3. See the article on Dee in Charles Henry Cooper and Thompson Cooper, *Athenae Cantabrigienses*, 2 vols., Cambridge, 1858 and 1861, II, 497-510, and the one in the *Dictionary of National Biography*; also Charlotte Fell-Smith, *John Dee*, London, 1909. Dee's own *A True & Faithful Relation of what passed for many Yeers between Dr. John Dee . . . and some Spirits*, London, 1659, is the second half of his diary, published by Meric Casaubon with an interesting preface; the first half, discovered later, still remains in manuscript. From the latter, Miss Fell-Smith, 84-86, quotes the "Faustian" passage referred to. For one of the many ways in which Goethe could have come to a knowledge of John Dee, see the third part of Friedrich Roth-Scholtz, *Deutsches Theatrvm Chemicvm*, Nürnberg, 1732, which contains his portrait, biography, and bibliography; see introduction 4-13, main text 3-5 and note, Dee's notes on Roger Bacon's *De Secretis Operibus Artis et Naturae*, 338-348, and the sections on and by Edward Kelley, 733-854.

4. E.g. (from Coopers' list): no. 46. *Atlantidis, vulgariter Indiae Occidentalis nominatae, emendatior descriptio . . .* , 1580, and no. 49. *De modo Evangelii Jesu Christi publicandi, propagandi, stabiliendi inter Infideles Atlanticos . . .* , 1581—these together with his researches for Queen Elizabeth into English colonial rights and his work and associations with the navigators and geographers (Gerard Mercator, Abraham Ortelius, and the great English navigators were personal friends of his); see Fell-Smith, esp. 8, 29, 38-44, 52-55, 66, 89, 237 f., 240 f.

5. The following two statements, one older, the other more modern, are characteristic. Johannes Niejahr, "Kritische Untersuchungen zu Goethes Faust," *Euphorion*, IV (1897), 272-287 and 489-508; p. 278: "Als Goethe begann 'Habe nun ach! Juristerei' [sic] stand er noch unter dem Einfluss des Puppenspiels, die traditionelle Gestalt des alten Zauberers schwebte ihm noch vor, der im Bann volkstümlich christlicher Vorstellungen, wenn auch in trotziger Auflehnung gegen sie (Vers 16), seine Seele dem Teufel verschreibt. Als er fortfuhr: 'O sähst du voller Mondenschein,' schritt er kühn aus den Grenzen der Sage hinaus, er war entschlossen, dem Stoff nur sein altes Kleid zu lassen, aber im übrigen

ihn ganz mit modernem Geist zu erfüllen und sein eigenes Herz-
blut in ihn überzuströmen." Similarly Witkowski II, 63: "Als
Goethe daran ging, die Faustsage in einer grossen Dichtung neu
zu gestalten, sie zum Gefäss seines Innenlebens zu machen, da
ergab sich für ihn notwendig eine wesentliche Umformung des
überlieferten Stoffes." Incidentally, the puppet plays recorded
after the appearance of the Goethean *Faust* often show the influence of the latter, and have no certain evidential value as to the
status of the Faust tradition during Goethe's boyhood and youth.

6. See the introduction and notes to Goebel's edition of the
first part of *Faust*, New York, 1907; also the important corrective
review by A. R. Hohlfeld, in the *Modern Language Review*, III
(1908), 379-392; likewise Goebel's article, "Goethes Quelle fuer
die Erdgeistscene [sic]," *The Journal of English and Germanic
Philology*, VIII (1909), 1-17. The Hohlfeld review has independent
value (even beyond the new material in it) as probably the best
informed and most judicious appraisal of the Neoplatonic and
Hermetic elements in Goethe's *Faust*.

Agnes Bartscherer, *Paracelsus, Paracelsisten und Goethes Faust
Eine Quellenstudie*, Dortmund, 1911 (review by Georg Wit-
kowski, *Literarisches Echo*, XIV, 1565 f.); *Zur Kenntnis des jungen
Goethe*, Dortmund, 1912.

Like Goebel and Bartscherer, Konrad Burdach also had a favorite prototype—in his case, Moses; like them he tried to make
too much out of a good idea, giving it a predominance it did not
deserve; on the positive side, from his broad background knowledge he also, like them, made a variety of valuable observations
far beyond his stated theme. With all his richness of resources
and his many cogent observations, there are some astounding
lapses of judgment and eccentricities of interpretation (compare
e.g. his treatment of Faust's last activity on earth with Hohlfeld's,
see ch. IV, note 16, below; also ch. II, notes 8 and 9) and his
works have to be used with great caution as well as gratitude. See
esp. his "Faust und Moses," *Sitzungsberichte der Königlich Preus-
sischen Akademie der Wissenschaften*, Jahrgang 1912, 358-403,
627-659, 736-789; also his "Faust und die Sorge," *Deutsche Viertel-
jahrsschrift für Literaturwissenschaft und Geistesgeschichte*, I
(1923), 1-60; "Die Disputationsszene und die Grundidee in Goethes Faust," *Euphorion*, XXVII (1926), 1-69; "Das religiöse Problem in Goethes Faust," *Euphorion*, XXXIII (1932), 3-83. Burdach
could be particularly misleading through basing his conclusions

on inferences assumed to be facts, and he was able to make far-fetched analogies sound convincing unless one paused to scrutinize them. Two typical examples in "Faust und Moses" are the unacceptable or all too indefinite analogies on p. 387 to "Wald und Höhle" and on p. 654 f. to the opening scene of the second part, the "Anmutige Gegend."

Like Moses, Hercules deserves some consideration as a prototype; for Goethe he was also laden with symbolic significance. Though we might hesitate to infer from the Hercules apotheosis in "Von deutscher Baukunst" that the young poet even then, during the period of the *Urfaust*, had envisioned the conclusion of the second part, Faust's ascent to heaven, nevertheless there may be a significant archetypal connection via the tradition of the Baroque apotheosis.

7. On this transformation of Platonism in the Renaissance, see e.g. Ernst Cassirer, *Individuum und Kosmos in der Philosophie der Renaissance*, Leipzig, Berlin, 1927, esp. p. 69 and note 1 quoting Ficino, and 179 f.; also Rudolf Allers' comment on the Ficino passage in his "Microcosmus," *Traditio*, II (1944), p. 391 and note 207; and Nesca A. Robb, *Neoplatonism of the Italian Renaissance*, London, 1935, esp. 37 f., 43, 67 f., 87. For another kind of transformation of Neoplatonism in the Renaissance, namely the affirmation of the validity of the world of appearances, see e.g. Denis Saurat, *Milton, Man and Thinker*, New York, 1925, p. 280, note; and cf. Cassirer, 47, 137, 179 f., for the broader Renaissance background; also Allers, 388, n. 202. In further supplement to Saurat, it should be observed that the factor of Stoicism is fully as important as that of the Cabala (indeed the latter derives from the former in many of the points here pertinent). Since Goethe very early had contact with both Stoic and Cabalistic thought, both of these traditions need to be considered far more seriously alongside his oft-discussed Neoplatonism. Any good book on the whole of the Stoic philosophy (not just on its ethical system) will show, on page after page, remarkably close parallels to Goethe's ways of thinking and to the contents and frame of reference of his *Faust*. E. Vernon Arnold's *Roman Stoicism*, Cambridge, 1911, for instance, offers an excellent introduction, with numerous references to the classical sources, many of which Goethe certainly or probably knew since early youth.

8. *Goethes Gespräche Gesamtausgabe*, Flodoard Frhr. von Biedermann ed., 5 vols., Leipzig, 1909-11 (hereafter referred to as

Biedermann); III, 79 (Feb. 26, 1824): "Ich schrieb meinen Götz von Berlichingen, sagte er, als junger Mensch von zweiundzwanzig und erstaunte zehn Jahre später über die Wahrheit meiner Darstellung. Erlebt und gesehen hatte ich bekanntlich dergleichen nicht, und ich musste also die Kenntnis mannigfaltiger menschlicher Zustände durch Antizipation besitzen."

9. *Ibid.* III, 81 (same date): "Mag sein, antwortete Goethe; allein hätte ich nicht die Welt durch Antizipation bereits in mir getragen, ich wäre mit sehenden Augen blind geblieben, und alle Erforschung und Erfahrung wäre nichts gewesen als ein ganz totes und vergebliches Bemühen. Das Licht ist da und die Farben umgeben uns; allein trügen wir kein Licht und keine Farben im eigenen Auge, so würden wir auch ausser uns dergleichen nicht wahrnehmen." (His famous quatrain, "Wär nicht das Auge sonnenhaft," dates from the previous year, 1823; and by the way, neither idea nor image was found by him first in Plotinus but much earlier in pre-Plotinian sources; see Arnold, 134, 139 f., and 249 f.) For a Renaissance parallel (or perhaps even source?) for his idea of "anticipation," of harmony of subject and object, in Patrizzi and Telesio, see Cassirer, *Individuum*, 156, last sentence, and f. See also Arnold, 130 f. for its Stoic sources.

10. *W.A.* IV, 2, 186 f.: "Sieh Lieber, was doch alles Schreibens Anfang und Ende ist: die Reproduktion der Welt um mich, durch die innere Welt die alles packt, verbindet, neuschafft, knetet und in eigner Form, Manier, wieder hinstellt—das bleibt ewig Geheimnis. . . .

". . . ich fordere das kritischste Messer auf, die bloss übersetzten Stellen [im Clavigo] abzutrennen vom Ganzen, ohne es zu zerfleischen. . . ." Cf. Biedermann IV, 103.

W.A. I, 37, 322: "Das Haften an eben der Gestalt unter *Einer* Lichtart muss notwendig den, der Auge hat, endlich in alle Geheimnisse leiten, wodurch sich das Ding ihm darstellt, wie es ist." And see end of note 9 above, and note 14 below.

11. *W.A.* I, 28, 98: "Faust war schon vorgerückt, Götz von Berlichingen baute sich nach und nach in meinem Geiste zusammen, das Studium des fünfzehnten und sechzehnten Jahrhunderts beschäftigte mich. . . ." See also *ibid.*, p. 52.

12. *W.A.* I, 35, 7: "Für mich war diese Bemühung nicht unfruchtbar; denn wie das Studium zu Berlichingen und Egmont mir tiefere Einsicht in das fünfzehnte und sechzehnte Jahrhundert gewährte, so musste mir diesmal die Verworrenheit des sieb-

zehnten sich, mehr als sonst vielleicht geschehen wäre, entwickeln."

13. Biedermann III, 152 f. (Jan. 10, 1825): "Ich schrieb den Egmont im Jahre 1775, also vor fünfzig Jahren. Ich hielt mich sehr treu an die Geschichte und strebte nach möglichster Wahrheit." (Cf. 340 on his changes in the figure of Egmont.)

14. *Ibid.* III, 253 and 254 (Jan. 29, 1826): " '. . . solange er [der Dichter] bloss seine wenigen subjektiven Empfindungen ausspricht, ist er noch keiner zu nennen; aber sobald er die Welt sich anzueignen und auszusprechen weiss, ist er ein Poet. Und dann ist er unerschöpflich und kann immer neu sein, wogegen aber eine subjektive Natur ihr bisschen Inneres bald ausgesprochen hat und zuletzt in Manier zugrunde geht. . . .'
" 'Jedes tüchtige Bestreben dagegen wendete sich aus dem Innern hinaus auf die Welt, wie Sie an allen grossen Epochen sehen, die wirklich im Streben und im Vorschreiten begriffen und alle objektiver Natur waren.'
"Die ausgesprochenen Worte gaben Anlass zu der geistreichsten Unterhaltung, wobei besonders der grossen Zeit des fünfzehnten und sechzehnten Jahrhunderts gedacht wurde."
See also, e.g. Goethe's great essay of 1797, "Der Versuch als Vermittler von Objekt und Subjekt," (*W.A.* II, 11, 21-37, esp. 21-24 and 27-31). Cassirer, *Individuum*, 170, aptly paraphrases the attitude of Leonardo da Vinci, for whom art and science were each "una seconda creazione": "Aber beide Schöpfungen erhalten ihren Wert eben dadurch, dass sie sich nicht von der Natur, von der empirischen Wahrheit der Dinge entfernen, sondern dass sie eben diese Wahrheit erfassen und aufdecken." Cf. 173. See also 47 f. and 61 for Nicolaus Cusanus' advocacy of the study of the outer world as the means toward an understanding of the inner world, and 96 summarizing Carolus Bovillus' conviction that knowledge of self can come only through knowledge of the world. And see below ch. VII, n. 6.

15. Biedermann III, 100 (April 14, 1824): "Meine ganze Zeit wich von mir ab, denn sie war ganz in subjektiver Richtung begriffen, während ich in meinem objektiven Bestreben im Nachteile und völlig allein stand." See also III, 143; IV, 79 f., 103, 251.

16. *Ibid.* I, 26 (Oct. 11, 1773): "In der Tat besitzt er, so weit ich ihn kenne, eine ausnehmend anschauende, sich in die Gegenstände durch und durch hineinfühlende Dichterkraft, so dass alles lokal und individuell in seinem Geiste wird."

17. The inadequacy of the knowledge of the Renaissance can be seen even in such an excellent article as Erich Schmidt's "Zur Vorgeschichte des Goethe'schen Faust. 2. Faust und das sechzehnte Jahrhundert," and ". . . iii. Johann Valentin Andreä," *Goethe-Jahrbuch*, iii (1882), 77-131, and iv (1883), 127-140. Schmidt's survey is the best of its day and is still decidedly worth reading for a number of particulars; but from it no valid judgment as to the Renaissance basis of the Goethean *Faust* could possibly be reached. Walther ·Rehm's brilliant early study, *Das Werden des Renaissancebildes in der deutschen Dichtung*, München, 1924, unfortunately appeared too soon to profit from the newer insights into the nature of the Renaissance. He still accepted the Burckhardt-C. F. Meyer picture as the norm and measuring stick, and thus missed completely what Goethe had in the way of insights above and beyond the century that followed him. Rehm, indeed, saw virtually no Renaissance traits in Goethe's works before the *Tasso*, nor could he have so long as he accepted the criteria of that schematic, conceptualist picture of "Renaissance man" which violated the living reality of the protean, polymorphic, transitional period of the fifteenth and sixteenth centuries. It is true that various attempts were made in the late eighteenth and early nineteenth century to revive certain realms of symbolism; but these all too often concentrated on occult and esoteric fields, such as Rosicrucianism, Masonry, hagiology, etc. The end result of these usually dilettantish efforts was to make the realm of symbol seem all the more unreal, remote from life, merely strange, and thoroughly unimportant.

18. See esp. Max Morris, *Goethe-Studien*, 2nd rev. ed., 2 vols., Berlin, 1902; i, 13-41: "Swedenborg im Faust." Julius Goebel's refutation of the Swedenborg hypothesis in his *Faust* commentary, 277, 282, 283, and esp. in his article (see note 6 above), 11, note. See also Agnes Bartscherer, *Paracelsus*, 61 ff., and *Zur Kenntnis*, 18 f., 22 f., 26-29, 89-91, etc.; Konrad Burdach, "Faust und Moses," 652 note, and his "Das religiöse Problem," 49 f.; and the Hohlfeld review (see note 6), 381 and 383.

The persistent return of the long-since banished ghosts can be seen in a number of commentaries, up to Reinhard Buchwald's *Führer durch Goethes Faustdichtung*, Stuttgart, 1942, p. 448, his commentary on line 484, the Earth Spirit speaking: " 'An meiner Sphäre lang gesogen': nach Swedenborg hat jeder Geist eine Sphäre (Atmosphäre) um sich. Dass der genialisch machtvolle

147

Mensch an der Sphäre des Geistes 'saugt,' ist Goethes Erdichtung. Bei Swedenborg 'saugen' umgekehrt manche Geister am Haupt des Menschen." That hardly accords with our best knowledge; Goethe did not have to (and certainly did not) invent his expression by imagining the contrary of this repulsive vampire image; he could (and probably did) find the *direct* image in Paracelsus of a man exercising attraction and suction upon spiritual spheres, as Goebel had already pointed out in 1908 (his article, 11) and Bartscherer had confirmed in a variant quotation (*Zur Kenntnis*, 23). I have found both "attractio" and "suctio" in the direct Goethean use in Benedict Figulus, *Pandora Magnalium Naturalium*, Strassburg, 1608, sign. * (8v) and ** (iv, r & v), "Was aber nun der Mensch vom Gestirn sauget. . . ." See below ch. VII, n. 2, for fuller quotations from Figulus. The other supposed Swedenborg analogies are just as petty and particular, a few are just as farfetched, and none are very enlightening.

What has enabled the Swedenborg illusion to persist so long is perhaps the failure to draw the proper conclusions from the well-established fact that everything which Goethe could have obtained from him for his *Faust*, he already knew in better context and more vivid expression from his earlier readings in the Renaissance and classical writers. For proper perspective one must realize how derivative Swedenborg is, how much his works represent the fruits of reading rather than of revelation. A younger English contemporary of Goethe, William Blake (1757-1827), who was certainly well informed about such matters, said in *The Marriage of Heaven and Hell*, 1790 (with considerable impatience and hyperbole): "Any man of mechanical talents may, from the writings of Paracelsus or Jacob Behmen, produce ten thousand volumes of equal value with Swedenborg's." (Quoted in *The Letters of William Blake*, London [1906], p. 72 note.) Clear examples of the borrowings of Swedenborg are the passages on the planetary spirits which Morris cites (p. 15) as the sources for the apparition of the Earth Spirit. Not only are these related, directly or indirectly, to e.g. the "Colloqvivm Spiritvs Mercvrij et Monachi, Fratris Alberti Beyeri," first published in the *Alchimia Vera* of 1604 (see below, ch. VI, n. 25), but the latter offers far closer and more vivid parallels to Goethe's passage than do Swedenborg's pale derivatives.

This much influence the venerable scientist might have had on young Goethe, however: in the midst of the Age of Reason he

had dared publicly to assert his belief in and contact with the
spirit world; and the poet may well have been both pleased and
encouraged to find that an older man of established reputation
and European fame had also gone back to the spirit world of the
Renaissance and antiquity. All this might possibly have stimulated him to go on with those imaginings with which his brain
was already teeming.

19. Conveniently collected in Hans Gerhard Gräf, *Goethe über
seine Dichtungen*, part 2, vol. 2, Frankfurt, 1904, esp. 60 ff.; also
483 (Biedermann IV, 79, March 23, 1829): (Eckermann) "'. . . es
ist hübsch, wie er Sie treibt, und sehr liebenswürdig, wie er sich
durch seine Idee verleiten lässt, selber am Faust fortzuerfinden.
. . .'

"'Sie haben recht,' sagte Goethe, 'er war so, wie alle Menschen,
die zu sehr von der Idee ausgehen. . . . Ich hatte nur immer zu
tun, dass ich feststand und seine wie meine Sachen von solchen
Einflüssen freihielt und schützte.'"

20. Erwin Panofsky and Fritz Saxl, *Dürers 'Melencolia I', eine
quellen- und typengeschichtliche Untersuchung* (Studien der
Bibliothek Warburg, II), Leipzig, Berlin, 1923; and Panofsky,
Albrecht Dürer, 2 vols., Princeton, 1943, I, 156-171, and II, fig.
209-221. Franz Neubert, *Vom Doctor Faustus zu Goethes Faust*,
Leipzig, 1932, does have the "Melencolia I" as the first illustration,
with a general caption, but otherwise follows the well-trodden
paths.

21. For example, Goethe's reference to himself as an "Erd-
kulin" in his letter to Frau von Stein, May 19, 1776 (*W.A.* IV, 3,
62) is apparently the only evidence we have that he had read
Martin Montanus' *Das Ander theyl der Garten gesellschafft* (1558,
Cap. 5); see Ernst Martin, "Das Märchen vom Erdkühlein in
Goethes Briefen," *Goethe-Jahrbuch*, XIX (1898), 297-303; also XII
(1891), 289 and XX (1899), 275.

Goethe's *Ephemerides*, a reading notebook begun in 1770 in
Frankfurt and continued at Strassburg, is an example for a brief
span of time of the astounding range of his intellectual occupa-
tions (*W.A.* I, 37, 81-116, and notes in next vol.). If we only had,
in addition, a notebook of his readings for the spring of 1772, for
instance, when, as he says, he was occupied with the study of the
fifteenth and sixteenth centuries (see n. 11 above), the Renaissance
connections of *Faust* would, no doubt, long since have been obvious. A list of his readings for the whole period 1770-1775, instead

of only the occasional notes for the first year of this period, would offer overwhelming evidence. But we should be grateful for the lucky accident which preserved for us the few months of record we have, for they are sufficient to show how industrious, purposeful, and far-ranging young Goethe was in his reading—how remote from the trifling, convivial, only superficially intellectual youth that some biographers have put before us.

Another important section of young Goethe's background of reading would be opened up to scholars by the publication of the catalogue of his father's library. Through the courtesy of Professor F. H. Reinsch of the University of California at Los Angeles, I was able to examine a copy of the manuscript list after the completion of this study. It was most gratifying to note the many points at which it further substantiates hypotheses or conclusions of mine which were arrived at in other ways. Those books from the library which he reserved and had sent to him at Weimar are described in Hellmuth von Maltzahn's article, "Bücher aus dem Besitz des Vaters in Goethes Weimarer Bibliothek," *Jahrbuch des Freien Deutschen Hochstifts*, 1927, 363-382. The printing of a catalogue of Goethe's entire Weimar library was announced for 1909, but did not progress beyond mere beginnings. Even the autograph book list of 1788 has apparently never been published. Making this material generally available (all of it and not just those parts which fall in with certain favorite theories) would seem to be an obvious preliminary to any study of Goethe's intellectual antecedents and associations. New vistas into the poet's mind would be opened up to the critic who would be willing to weigh and sift carefully, relating external to internal evidence. However, negative conclusions from the absence of certain books cannot be drawn since young Goethe is known to have used the Frankfurt city library, for instance, and of course he had access to many a great private library.

22. To give just two early examples, there is his outburst near the end of "Zum Schäkespears Tag" beginning (*W.A.* 1, 37, 134): "Und was will sich unser Jahrhundert unterstehen von Natur zu urteilen?" And in "Nach Falkonet und über Falkonet" he contrasts the paper civilization of his own day with the artistic substantiality of Renaissance and Baroque; he is speaking (*ibid.*, 318) of the man of fashion "der sich an der Flitterherrlichkeit der neuen Welt ergötzt": "Alle Quellen natürlicher Empfindung, die der Fülle unsrer Väter offen waren, schliessen sich ihm. Die

papierne Tapete, die an seiner Wand in wenig Jahren verbleicht,
ist ein Zeugnis seines Sinns und ein Gleichnis seiner Werke." Then
follows the contrast in Raphael, Rubens, and Rembrandt. See also
e.g. in "Von deutscher Baukunst" (*ibid.*, 142) and the poem to
Merck accompanying his *Götz*, "Schicke dir hier in altem Kleid"
(*W.A.* 1, 4, 195 f.), esp. "Das Alt die jungen Schläuch reisst gar,"
and following.
23. Letter to Carl Ludwig von Knebel, Nov. 14, 1827 (*W.A.*
IV, 43, 167): ". . . die Hauptintention ist klar und das Ganze
deutlich; auch das Einzelne wird es sein und werden, wenn man
die Teile nicht an sich betrachten und erklären, sondern in Be-
ziehung auf das Ganze sich verdeutlichen mag."

II. THREE PRELIMINARY EXAMPLES:
WAGNER, MEPHISTOPHELES, AND THE
AERIAL SPIRITS

1. *Individuum und Kosmos*, 15 f.
2. Lines 534-537:

"Wenn ihr's nicht fühlt, ihr werdet's nicht erjagen,
Wenn es nicht aus der Seele dringt
Und mit urkräftigem Behagen
Die Herzen aller Hörer zwingt. . . ."

W.A. 1, 37, 314: "Jede Form, auch die gefühlteste, hat etwas Un-
wahres; allein sie ist ein- für allemal das Glas, wodurch wir die
heiligen Strahlen der verbreiteten Natur an das Herz der Menschen zum Feuerblick sammeln. Aber das Glas! Wems nicht ge-
geben wird, wirds nicht erjagen; es ist, wie der geheimnisvolle
Stein der Alchymisten, Gefäss und Materie, Feuer und Kühlbad."
For parallel sentiments in Petrarch that knowledge must be assimilated to life and become integrally related to the human personality and its expressive creative life, see Robb, 28 f. Various discerning humanists saw the fallacy of formalism; Melanchthon,
for instance, took care to make his position clear in the introduc-
tory section of his *Elementorum Rhetorices Libri Duo* (*Opera*, ed.
Bretschneider, XIII, Halle, 1846, e.g. col. 418): "Nam ad bene
dicendum in primis requiritur perfecta earum rerum cognitio, de
quibus oratio instituitur. Insania est enim, non eloquentia, de

rebus ignotis et incompertis dicere." But for the completely anti-formalist attitude see esp. Bartscherer, *Paracelsus*, 314-317.

3. A good first acquaintance with some of these Wagners among the humanists, estimable and industrious men, can be made in John Edwin Sandys, *A History of Classical Scholarship*, 3 vols., Cambridge, 1903-08, esp. in vol. ii.

4. See esp. Charles Schmidt, *Michael Schütz genannt Toxites. Leben eines Humanisten und Arztes aus dem 16. Jahrhundert*, Strassburg, 1888; also the supplement to the bibliography in Karl Sudhoff's "Ein Beitrag zur Bibliographie der Paracelsisten im 16. Jahrhundert," *Zentralblatt für Bibliothekswesen*, x (1893), 325 f.

5. See esp. Robb, 163-175, and the English translation of the verse passages, 291-295. Only after the completion of this section did I succeed in gaining access to Vincenzo Jovine's interesting study "L'Astarotte di L. Pulci e il Mefistofele di W. Goethe," *Rendiconti della Reale Accademia dei Lincei, classe di scienze morali, storiche e filologiche*, Serie Quinta, vol. xvii (Roma, 1908), 483-517 (and see the report in the *Literarisches Echo*, xi [1908-09], col. 1559 f.). Though Jovine brings out, in far greater detail than I do, both the similarities and differences between the two demons, he does not with one word suggest the relation of Pulci and his demon to the "Faustian" elements in the Medicean circle, which to my mind is the most important factor. The author exposes the diabolic characteristics and intentions underlying Astarotte's affable helpfulness and reasonableness, and shows that for all his penetration he too had, like Mephistopheles, an intellectual blind spot by which ironically his latent evil is turned to the service of ultimate good. Even though Jovine in a note (500 f.) cites Francesco Novati, *Attraverso il medio evo*, Bari, 1905, on the long background in legend and folklore of such mixed spirits of evil and good, in the text and in the summary (515 f.) he insists exclusively that Pulci and Goethe proceeded subjectively, going against tradition to create a milder and more human kind of devil in conformity to their own conciliatory spirits: ". . . Astarotte e Mefistofele sono i fedeli interpreti d'una parte dello spirito del Pulci e del Goethe." The fifth and last point of his summary, however, is well taken: "Messi finalmente nell'identica posizione d'esser guida dell'uomo, per voluntà e per impegno, mentre cercano di perdere e traviare, riescono nell'intento opposto e operano, senza volerlo, del bene, ubbidendo ineluttabilmente ai fini della Provvidenza." With Goe-

the's knowledge and love of Italian literature from childhood onward through his life, Jovine considers it likely that he had read Pulci.

6. Cf. Robb, 165 f. and 291 f., with *Faust*, lines 11612 ff., esp. 11659 f. and 11666 ff.

7. See Goethe's diary for August 11, 1827 (*W.A.* III, 11, 96): "*Canti Carnascialeschi* nach langer Zeit wieder angesehen. Herrlichstes Denkmal der florentinischen Epoche unter Lorenz Medicis." (correct text "unter" not "und," cf. index of *W.A.*). A previous reading had occurred in the 1790's in connection with his Cellini translation, as we can gather with certainty from Goethe's discussion of both Lorenzo's serious and comic poems in the appended notes (*W.A.* I, 44, 347). Whether he had also read them earlier in the 1770's, we do not know; it would not be at all surprising if he had.

8. Mephistopheles is indeed far more tricky in his subtly calculated twists and deflections; and the misinterpretations of *Faust* that have resulted from too simple a faith in his words would have delighted that son of chaos. Burdach, for instance, believed that Faust's newly won lands would be inundated upon his death ("Das religiöse Problem," pp. 26 and 36). After observing one group of *Faust* scholars especially (the negativists) succumbing so easily to Mephisto's trickery, one's admiration for the mental strength of ex-Professor Faust, who had him as a constant companion, must rise enormously.

9. Some of the critical uncertainty about Mephistopheles, the aerial spirits, and the Earth Spirit is neatly epitomized by Burdach, "Das religiöse Problem," p. 18: "Selbst die innigsten Bewunder der Herrlichkeit des Goethischen Faustdramas können sich nicht täuschen über dieses künstlerische Gebrechen: das Schwanken und die daraus entstandene Unklarheit in der Darstellung der Natur Mephistos, des Erdgeists, der Elementargeister." Ironically it is precisely with regard to these three matters that the shortcomings have been far less Goethe's in presentation than the critics' in understanding. They may be symptomatic of the inadequacies of the traditional approach to *Faust*.

10. See Gräf, 484 f., note, for Laroche's report on Goethe's coaching, and 507, note, on Karl von Holtei's description of the performance: "Er hielt streng die Weisung inne, die im Gedichte vorliegt, und blieb durchweg der humoristisch-negierende, witzig-spöttelnde, lustig-zweifelnde, listig-spähende *Geist*. Im Einklange

damit standen seine Geberden, sein vornehm-freies Betragen, seine meisterlich-schlichte Rede, worin weder stark betont, noch wichtig herausgehoben, noch effecthascherisch gedehnt, sondern immer flüssig, eindringlich, verständlich und nach Hamlets Vorschrift 'leicht von der Zunge weg' gesprochen wurde. Sein Mephistopheles war kein Teufel von Fleisch und Bein, der herumläuft wie der brüllende Löwe und sieht, welchen er verschlinge. Es war eine symbolische Erscheinung, die auf der Höhe des Gedichtes stand."

11. Biedermann III, 152, to Captain Hutton, Jan. 10, 1825, as reported by Eckermann: "So der Charakter des Mephistopheles ist durch die Ironie und als lebendiges Resultat einer grossen Weltbetrachtung wieder etwas sehr Schweres."

12. See Hesiod, *Works and Days*, lines 122 f. and 141 f. In three of the main philosophic faiths which arose, the Pythagorean, the Platonic, and the Stoic, this system of spirits was retained, though variously developed and interpreted. It was transmitted by such popular philosophers as Cicero, Plutarch, and Apuleius, as well as by the poets. See Plutarch, "On the Cessation of the Oracles," section x, and "Of the Face which Appears on the Orb of the Moon," sections xxviii and xxx. And see Arnold, 232 and n. 100, 264 and n. 139 f. (in the Stoic system evil became a mere subsidiary instrumentality of the Divine purpose; thus there were no truly evil spirits). A Renaissance poet who combined ancient and contemporary speculations about the aerial spirits in an unorthodox fashion was Marcellus Palingenius (Stellatus) in his *Zodiacus Vitae*, Venice, ca. 1531 (numerous reprints and translations), esp. in Books vii, viii, and xii (anon. English translation, privately printed, n.p., 1896, 153 ff., 177 f., 246, 288, 291).

13. See Hanns Bächtold-Stäubli, *Handwörterbuch des deutschen Aberglaubens*, 10 vols., Berlin and Leipzig, 1927-42, article "Fee," and especially in vol. ix, supplement, the article "singen," "B. Gesang der Dämonen und Geister," col. 463 and 481.

14. *Ibid.*, article on "Paracelsus," col. 1397, "Die Elementarwesen." Paracelsus' ideas on the elementals are to be found especially in his *Liber Meteororum* and his *Liber de Nymphis, Sylphis, Pygmaeis et Salamandris, et de Caeteris Spiritibus*.

15. Henricus Cornelius Agrippa von Nettesheim, *De Occvlta Philosophia Libri Tres*, first published at Antwerp and Paris in 1531, Cologne, 1533; see esp. Book iii, ch. 16, 32, 34 and 35, and Book i, ch. 39.

16. First English translation, London, 1651: reprint of Book 1, New York, 1897, quotation on p. 123 f.

17. Included e.g. in the copy of the *Opera* in Northwestern University Library, Lugduni, n.d. (later sixteenth century); see esp. 452, passage beginning, "Est aliud genus spirituum . . . non adeo noxium, hominibus proximum. . . ."

18. It is strange that R. Kienast, in his fine study, *Johann Valentin Andreae und die vier echten Rosenkreutzer-Schriften*, Leipzig, 1926, was puzzled by this passage in the *Fama Fraternitatis des löblichen Ordens des Rosenkreutz* and attempted a far-fetched explanation which is obviously untenable. See his study, 101 and 117 f. Will-Erich Peuckert's great study, *Die Rosenkreuzer*, Jena, 1928, which I read some eight years ago, was unfortunately not available to me for comparison on this detail.

19. English translation, London, 1680, reprinted New York and London, 1914, 179 ff. The Paracelsus passage on which this is based is quoted in Bartscherer, *Zur Kenntnis*, 87 f.

20. Biedermann IV, 473 (conversation with Johann Daniel Falk): ". . . oder wenn sie [die Leser] in der Fortsetzung von Faust etwa zufällig an die Stelle kämen, wo der Teufel selbst Gnad' und Erbarmen vor Gott findet; das, denke ich doch, vergeben sie mir sobald nicht!" Cf. Gräf, 226, who dates the conversation tentatively June 21, 1816. Goethe's intentional and purposeful unorthodoxy in his treatment of the supernatural comes out especially clearly here, as does also his amusement at the way the German and French critics by the very act of straining to get the point had missed it completely, and had even demanded that certain parts be revised to conform to their sense of the fitness of things. On Goethe's early knowledge of the heretical doctrine that the devils might be saved, see Bartscherer, *Zur Kenntnis*, 100 f. Cf. also Wieland's report, Biedermann I, 134 (omitted in Gräf).

21. It seems never to have been noticed that Faust's Helena has taken over some of the attributes of the beautiful fays beloved and tragically lost by the noble heroes of medieval romance.

22. Robb, 292 f.; Italian original, 170:

> ". . . non vengon costretti
> Nell'aqua o nello specchio, e in aria stanno
> Mostrando sempre falsitate e inganno.

Vannosi l'un con l'altro poi vantando
D'aver fatto parer quel che non sia
Chi si diletta ir gli uomini gabbando
Chi si diletta di filosofia
Chi venire i tesori rivelando
Chi del futuro dir qualche bugia
Si ch'io t'ho letto un gentil mio quaderno
Chè gentilezza è bene anche in inferno."

23. Most conveniently together in Gräf, 233 f. and 327. The exact date of the latter is unknown; Biedermann (IV, 305 f.) puts it as late as 1829-30.

24. To my knowledge, this relation of *The Tempest* to *Dr. Faustus* was first suggested by R. A. Redford, in his "Shakespeare and the Faust Legend," *Gentleman's Magazine*, 285 (1898), 547-566. It seems to have escaped the attention of all *Faust* scholars (the reference to John Dee is my addition). Recently the relation of *The Tempest* to the Goethean *Faust* was freshly examined by G. F. Hartlaub, in his *Prospero und Faust Ein Beitrag zum Problem der schwarzen und weissen Magie*, Dortmund, 1948, though this supplements rather than supersedes the Redford article.

25. See his letter of February 13, 1769 to Friederike Oeser (*W.A.* IV, 1, 189) : ". . . dass ich eben so gerne die Zeit über hätte in einen gespaltenen Baum wollen eingezaubert sein." This frequently overlooked allusion to the plight of Ariel is quite different from the Shakespeare quotations in other youthful letters, where the source was the popular anthology of William Dodd, *The Beauties of Shakespeare*. Wieland's translation of *The Tempest* appeared in vol. 2 of his *Shakespear Theatralische Werke*, 8 vols., Zürich, 1762-66, though Goethe was, of course, by that time well able to read the play in the original. Cf. Bartscherer, *Zur Kenntnis*, 10-13; and see James Boyd, *Goethe's Knowledge of English Literature*, Oxford, 1932, 58, for other allusions to the play from a few years later. It should be added that his father's library contained not only the Wieland translation but also the English edition of 1714. There has always been a tendency to minimize Goethe's knowledge of Shakespeare before Strassburg despite his own earlier statement of February 20, 1770. This was misplaced by Boyd on p. 17, n. 2, and actually contradicts his assertions on p. xiv and 16 f. For a more judicious account see Lawrence Marsden Price, *The Reception of English Literature in Germany*, Berkeley, 1932, 297-299.

26. *W.A.* 1, 16, 102:

> "Doch das schmerzt mich nur,
> Dass ich die tiefe Kenntnis der Natur
> Mit Müh geforscht und leider! nun vergebens;
> Dass hohe Menschenwissenschaft,
> Manche geheimnisvolle Kraft,
> Mit diesem Geist der Erd entschwinden soll."

III. FAUST'S INTELLECTUAL POSITION:
CUSANUS, PICO DELLA MIRANDOLA, AND OTHERS

1. This poem is effectively buried in the critical apparatus to the *Fastnachtspiele aus dem fünfzehnten Jahrhundert*, Heinrich Adelbert von Keller ed., *Bibliothek des literarischen Vereins in Stuttgart*, xxx (1853), 1152-1157. It was printed at an early date (exact date unknown), and there is at least one manuscript version of it, in the Dresden codex, which Keller here published. For the reference to this, I am indebted to Professor William S. Heckscher of the State University of Iowa (see *Art Bulletin*, xxxi, 1, March 1949, 67). Quotations of some of the key passages follow:

> "Der hellisch vogt hat nye mer gefangen
> Dann jn dem mussig gannge vnd jn tragkeit
> Vnd wenn der sunder velt in zagheit
> An den zweyen ennden vecht er am meynsten
> Mit sein sel garn mit allen seinen geisten
>
> . . .
>
> Hette jch gelernt jn allen schuln
> Vnd were doctor in medicinis [sic]
> Vnd in theoloya nicht minus
> Vnd ein hoher philozophus
> Vnd were ein bewertter medicus
>
> . . .
>
> Vnd hette lerjare gedint den dreyen
> Noch konde jch nicht so wol ertzneyen
> Als wenn der erbeyter einen tropffen switzt
> So er an seiner erbeyt erhitzt
>
> . . .

Dorumb ist erbeyt der gotlichts orden
So er ye auf erden gestifft ist worden
. . .
So lasse dich nymmer mussig vinden
Wiewol die zagheit bleibt dahinden."

The Dresden version, in Keller, is corrupted in the second line of the review of the faculties, "Vnd were doctor in medicinis," which should obviously concern the doctor of laws (theology, philosophy, and medicine following); the lack of the proper rhyme word here also indicates the corruption. No other version was available to me. On Paracelsus' disparaging references to the faculties, see Bartscherer, *Paracelsus*, 28 ff.; see also her *Zur Kenntnis*, 74, and preceding pages from 62.

2. See above ch. I, n. 20.

3. Cassirer, *Individuum*, 53 ff., esp. 57-60. Though there is not one specific reference to *Faust* in the whole book (only one to the "Faustian" mood of striving and its philosophical basis in the Renaissance, 73 f.), Cassirer evidently found Goethean formulations so apt for expressing Renaissance problems, attitudes, and interrelations, that again and again in the text we find phrases and paraphrases from *Faust* not indicated by quotation marks or otherwise (e.g. 58, 156, 201). There seems to be in his thought a tacit assumption at least that Goethe's Faust moved in the intellectual and spiritual atmosphere of that period even though, to my knowledge, he never made a direct statement to that effect.

4. Edward McCurdy, *Leonardo da Vinci's Note-Books*, New York, 1935, 8-11.

5. Ernst Cassirer, "Giovanni Pico della Mirandola," *Journal of the History of Ideas*, III (1942), 123-144 and 319-346. The summary is based chiefly on 327-342 and also on 138-140. It will be observed that I follow Cassirer's exposition very closely, often to the point of direct quotation, even though in different sequence. The concluding direct quotations are from 320 f., 323 f., and 330 f.

6. *Petrarca, Valla, Ficino, Pico, Pomponazzi, Vives The Renaissance Philosophy of Man*, ed. by Ernst Cassirer, Paul Oskar Kristeller, John Herman Randall, Jr., and others, Chicago, 1948, 224 f., 227, and 247-249. The translation of Pico's oration is by Elizabeth Livermoore Forbes. For the setting of his exposition of magic, see Cassirer, *Individuum*, 178 f.

IV. THE DIVERSITY OF
RENAISSANCE PROTOTYPES AND MOTIFS

1. Cassirer, "Pico," 126.
2. John Addington Symonds, ed. and transl., *The Sonnets of Michael Angelo Buonarroti and Tommaso Campanella*, London, 1878, 170. The Italian text:

> "Ben sei mila anni in tutto 'l mondo io vissi:
> Fede ne fan l'istorie delle genti,
> Ch'io manifesto agli uomini presenti
> Co' libri filosofici ch'io scrissi. . . ."

See Giovanni Papini's edition of *Le Poesie*, Lanciano, 1913, I, 150.
3. *W.A.* IV, 41, 202 (to Carl Wilhelm von Humboldt, Oct. 22, 1826): "Es ist eine meiner ältesten Konzeptionen, sie ruht auf der Puppenspielüberlieferung, dass Faust den Mephistopheles genötigt, ihm die Helena zum Beilager heranzuschaffen. Ich habe von Zeit zu Zeit daran fortgearbeitet, aber abgeschlossen konnte das Stück nicht werden als in der Fülle der Zeiten, da es denn jetzt seine volle 3000 Jahre spielt, von Trojas Untergang bis zur Einnahme von Missolunghi. Dies kann man also auch für eine Zeiteinheit rechnen, im höheren Sinne." Similarly to J. S. M. (Sulpiz) Boisserée (*ibid.*, 209, same date): "Die Helena ist eine meiner ältesten Konzeptionen, gleichzeitig mit Faust, immer nach *einem* Sinne, aber immer um- und umgebildet. Was zu Anfang des Jahrhunderts fertig war, liess ich Schiller sehen, der, wie unsere Korrespondenz ausweist, mich treulich aufmunterte, fortzuarbeiten. Das geschah auch; aber abgerundet konnte das Stück nicht werden als in der Fülle der Zeiten, da es denn jetzt seine volle dreitausend Jahre spielt, vom Untergange Trojas bis auf die Zerstörung Missolunghis, phantasmagorisch freilich, aber mit reinster Einheit des Orts und der Handlung." See also his letter to Nees von Esenbeck, May 25, 1827 (*ibid.*, 42, 197 f.).

I include the reference to the Faust puppet play since it affords an excellent instance of the slightness of the relation of the pre-Goethean to the Goethean Faust.

4.   "Wer nicht von dreitausand Jahren
      Sich weiss Rechenschaft zu geben,

Bleib im Dunkeln unerfahren,
Mag von Tag zu Tage leben."

From the poem, "Und wer franzet oder britet," Buch des Unmuts
(*W.A.* 1, 6, 110). No one previously seems to have noticed the
relation of Goethe's lines to Campanella's. Campanella's "six thousand years" is, of course, based on the conventional chronology
from the creation of the world, expressed in round numbers.
Goethe's "three thousand years" is conditioned by the *Helena*
drama (Act III), and does not fully encompass Acts II and V. For
another Renaissance parallel, which does speak of three thousand
years of perspective, see the quotation from a Ficino letter in Robb,
73, n. 1; pages 72-74 vividly illustrate the relation of this thought
to the dynamic expansive impulse of the Renaissance, and indicate the noble philanthropy that is to be the ultimate result.

5. Symonds, 27. Luigi Tansillo, *Il Canzoniere*, ed. by Erasmo
Pèrcopo, vol. 1, Napoli, 1926, 5 f. (see also the footnote referring
to Benedetto Croce's study of this sonnet; also Croce's *Problemi
di Estetica*):

"Poi che spiegate ho l'ale al bel desio,
quanto per l'alte nubi altier lo scorgo,
piú le superbe penne al vento porgo,
e, d'ardir colmo, verso il ciel l'invio.
Né del figliuol di Dedalo il fin rio
fa ch'io paventi, anzi via piú risorgo:
ch'io cadrò morto a terra ben m'accorgo;
ma qual vita s'agguaglia al morir mio?

La voce del mio cor per l'aria sento:
—Ove mi porti, temerario? China,
ché raro è senza duol troppo ardimento!—
—Non temer (rispond'io) l'alta rovina,
poiché tant'alto sei, mori contento,
se 'l ciel sí illustre morte ne destina.—"

Bruno's version in *Gli Eroici Furori* shows many changes (quoted
in Cassirer, *Individuum*, 200, as being by Bruno). There is much
else in this dialogue, as well as in Bruno's other works that helps
to elucidate the Goethean *Faust*. I have unfortunately not seen
Werner Saenger's *Goethe und Giordano Bruno. Ein Beitrag zur
Geschichte der Goethischen Weltanschauung*, Germanische Stu-

dien, Heft 91, Berlin, 1930 (review by Franz Koch, *Euphorion*, XXXIII, 1932, 204-207).

6. *The Works of Edmund Spenser A Variorum Edition*, ed. by Edwin Greenlaw, Charles Grosvenor Osgood, Frederick Morgan Padelford, and Ray Heffner, 4 vols. in 10, Baltimore, 1932-49: *The Minor Poems Volume Two* (1947), 225 and commentary 446 f., which also contains the Italian text of Tasso's sonnet. Angelo Solerti ed., *Le Rime*, 4 vols., Bologna, 1898-1902, II, 98, no. 67:

"L'alma vaga di luce e di bellezza
Ardite spiega al ciel l'ale amorose,
Ma sí le fa l'umanità gravose
Che le dechina a quel ch'in terra apprezza.

E de' piaceri a la dolce esca avvezza
Ove in sereno volto Amor la pose
Tra bianche perle e mattutine rose
Par che non trovi altra maggior dolcezza;

E fa quasi augellin ch'in alto s'erga
E poi discenda al fin ov'altri il cibi,
E quasi volontario s'imprigioni;

E fra tanti del ciel graditi doni
Sí gran diletto par che in voi delibi
Ch'in voi solo si pasce e solo alberga."

Cf. *Faust*, lines 1074 ff., esp. 1112 ff.; also 640-643.

7. *W.A.* III, 1, 43 and IV, 3, 246; to Frau von Stein, Sept. 8, 1778: "Setzte mich an mein Küchenfeuer und las den Cardan wieder einmal, mit vieler Freude und Rührung." Compare *Dichtung und Wahrheit* (I, 26, 11 f.) with Cardanus, *De Vita Propria Liber*, ch. II (English transl. by Jean Stoner, New York, 1930, 4-6). Goethe's later reference to the reading of Cardanus, Nov. 1, 4, and 5, 1808 (III, 3, 396) probably does not concern the autobiography but the *De Subtilitate*, as can be seen from the accompanying reading of Julius Caesar Scaliger, who attacked that book in his *Exotericarvm Exercitationvm Liber XV. De Svbtilitate, Ad Hieronymvm Cardanvm*, var. ed. His last reference to Cardanus, in connection with Francis Bacon, comes Jan. 28, 1809 (III, 4, 7).

8. *W.A.* II, 3, 218: "Cardan gehört unter diejenigen Menschen, mit denen die Nachwelt nie fertig wird, über die sie sich nicht leicht im Urteil vereinigt. . . . Er kannte sein eigenes Naturell bis auf einen gewissen Grad, doch konnte er bis ins höchste Alter

nicht darüber Herr werden. Gar oft haben wir bei ihm, seiner
Umgebung und seinem Bestreben, an Cellini denken müssen, um
so mehr, als beide gleichzeitig gelebt."

9. The first reference is obvious and well known, his letter to
Schiller's wife, April 21, 1798 (*W.A.* IV, 13, 123), where he speaks
of "die Schwierigkeit, den alten geronnenen Stoff wieder ins
Schmelzen zu bringen." "Ich habe nun auf cellinische Weise ein
Schock zinnerne Teller und eine Portion hartes trocknes Holz
dran gewendet. . . ." The second has no such direct allusion, but
the metaphor is clear and the reference probable; he writes to
Sulpiz Boisserée, Nov. 22, 1826 (*W.A.* IV, 41, 234): "Da der Guss
nach dem so lange studierten Modell endlich geglückt ist, so
wird nun des Ausführens und Ziselierens kein Ende."

10. *W.A.* I, 44, 350, 355-358, 361 (see also 345, 348, and 411 near
end):

"In einer so regsamen Stadt zu einer so bedeutenden Zeit
erschien ein Mann, der als Repräsentant seines Jahrhunderts und
vielleicht als Repräsentant sämtlicher Menschheit gelten dürfte.
Solche Naturen können als geistige Flügelmänner angesehen
werden, die uns mit heftigen Äusserungen dasjenige andeuten,
was durchaus, obgleich oft nur mit schwachen unkenntlichen
Zügen, in jeden menschlichen Busen eingeschrieben ist."

"Was uns jedoch aus seiner ganzen Geschichte am lebhaftesten
entgegenspringt, ist die entschieden ausgesprochene, allgemeine
Eigenschaft des Menschencharakters, die augenblickliche lebhafte
Gegenwirkung, wenn sich irgendetwas dem Sein oder dem Wollen
entgegensetzt."

"Wie aber die menschliche Natur sich immer ganz herzustellen
und darzustellen genötigt ist, so erscheint in diesen wüsten, sinn-
lichen Welträumen an unserm Helden sowie an seinen Um-
gebungen ein sittliches und religiöses Streben, das erste im gröss-
ten Widerspruch mit der leidenschaftlichen Natur, das andere
zu Beruhigung in verdienten und unverdienten unausweichlichen
Leiden.

"Unserm Helden schwebt das Bild sittlicher Vollkommenheit
als ein unerreichbares beständig vor Augen. Wie er die äussere
Achtung von andern fordert, ebenso verlangt er die innere von
sich selbst."

"Nicht weniger treibt ihn die Glaubenslehre seiner Kirche,
sowie die drang- und ahnungsvolle Zeit zu dem Wunderbaren."

"Bei einem festen Glauben an ein unmittelbares Verhältnis zu einer göttlichen und geistigen Welt, in welchem wir das Künftige voraus zu empfinden hoffen dürfen, musste er die Wunderzeichen verehren, in denen das sonst so stumme Weltall bei Schicksalen ausserordentlicher Menschen seine Teilnahme zu äussern scheint." "Aber nicht allein mit den obern Mächten bringt ihn sein wunderbares Geschick in Verhältnis; Leidenschaft und Übermut haben ihn auch mit den Geistern der Hölle in Berührung gesetzt." Some of these Cellini analogues were found long ago by Burdach in his search for Moses references and were pointed out by him. With his special purpose in mind, he naturally omitted others of importance and did not indicate the significance of the whole.

11. *W.A.* I, 44, 345 (compare with *Faust*, line 4040): ". . . so hoffte seine [Cosimos] tiefe Natur in der auflebenden Platonischen Philosophie den Aufschluss manches Rätsels. . . ."

12. Anton Reichl, "Goethes Faust und Agrippa von Nettesheim," *Euphorion*, IV (1897), 287-301; and see Bartscherer's critique and additions in her *Paracelsus*, 23-25.

13. See above ch. I, n. 3; Fell-Smith, 84-86.

14. *W.A.* I, 27, 203-205, 208, 217 and 320 f. But Herder's knowledge of young Goethe's trains of thought and his hostile reaction to them can be seen somewhat later in his letter to Merck in 1772, where he calls Goethe an "elenden Wahrsager, Naturkenner und Zeichendeuter." Quoted in Bartscherer, *Paracelsus*, 230.

15. Introduction, sign. a4; copy in the New York Society Library (from the Winthrop family). On Starkey see *Winthrop Papers*, ed. by Allyn B. Forbes, Massachusetts Historical Society, V (1947), 241 f.; John Langdon Sibley, *Biographical Sketches of Graduates of Harvard University*, I (Cambridge, Mass., 1873), 131-137; and the notes on Starkey in George Lyman Kittredge's "Dr. Robert Child the Remonstrant," *Publications of the Colonial Society of Massachusetts*, XXI (1919), 1-146, esp. 100 f. and notes, 132 and 134 ff. The account of Starkey in the *Dictionary of National Biography* is quite misleading; the *Errata* volume of 1904 corrects some but not all of the mistakes. There are a few additional facts in the present writer's *The First Century of New England Verse*, Worcester, Mass., American Antiquarian Society, 1944, 45 f. and 260.

The whole Eirenaeus Philalethes problem is very complex (he is not to be confused with "Eugenius Philalethes," who was Thomas Vaughan). Kittredge never published his more complete results, and I cannot be sure that I now have assembled most of the evidence he had. I agreed with him in identifying Starkey with this "Cosmopolite," until I found statements in the Winthrop Papers which suggest that yet another man might have been this mysterious adept, and that in the matter of authorship at least, Starkey's highly imaginative story about Eirenaeus Philalethes might have some grain of truth to it. A statement of Johannes Baptista van Helmont that has been hitherto overlooked strengthens this new hypothesis.

16. A. R. Hohlfeld, "Zum irdischen Ausgang von Goethes Faustdichtung," *Goethe Vierteljahresschrift der Goethe-Gesellschaft*, 1 (1936), 263-289, esp. 271, 279 f. and 285, though naturally the emphasis is more on England than on the United States. The larger purpose of Hohlfeld's study was to make clear once and for all Goethe's own poetic intention in this vital scene by unrolling the background of Goethe's related interests, studies, and points of view at the time the scene took final form and was written down. The exposition makes the negative interpretation of this scene untenable.

17. Aside from the thirty odd mentioned in the course of the text, let the following serve as examples: Johann Trithemius, Franciscus Georgius, Leonhard Thurneysser, Raphael Eglinus, Johann Baptista Grosschedel von Aicha, Heinrich Nollius, Rudolph Goclenius Jr., Michael Potier, Francis Kett, John Cunningham of Preston, Simon Forman, Richard Napier, Henry Percy Earl of Northumberland and his circle (Thomas Harriot, Robert Hues, Walter Warner). Warning: for any judgment as to their "Faustian" correspondences, the biographical dictionaries and other reference works are generally valueless and frequently misleading. For example, the article on Heinrich Nollius in the *Allgemeine deutsche Biographie* is a mere uncritical rewording of the extremely erroneous and superficial account in Christian Gottlieb Jöcher's *Allgemeines Gelehrten-Lexicon*. All the accounts of Leonhard Thurneysser continue to be based on J. C. W. Möhsen's of 1783, and miss the main point completely; even the full-length biography by Günther Bugge, Berlin, 1943, is entirely oblivious to the poetic significance of his pre-Berlin works, as is Wolfgang Stammler, *Von der Mystik zum Barock*, Stuttgart, 1927, 421.

V. NATURE AND THE BOOK OF NOSTRADAMUS

1. Lines 377-379, 382-385:

> "Drum hab' ich mich der Magie ergeben,
> Ob mir durch Geistes Kraft und Mund
> Nicht manch Geheimnis würde kund. . . .
> Dass ich erkenne, was die Welt
> Im Innersten zusammenhält,
> Schau' alle Wirkungskraft und Samen,
> Und tu' nicht mehr in Worten kramen."

The term "Wirkungskraft und Samen" goes back to the Stoic "λόγος σπερματικός," "the seed power," "the seminal word," and is a favorite concept of the Renaissance natural philosophers. See below, ch. VII, n. 14 and esp. n. 16 for young Goethe's use of this terminology.

2. The five references to "Natur":

414 f.: "Statt der lebendigen Natur
Da Gott die Menschen schuf hinein. . . ."

423 ff.: "Und wenn Natur dich unterweist,
Dann geht die Seelenkraft dir auf,
Wie spricht ein Geist zum andern Geist."

437 f.: ". . . [diese Zeichen, die] mit geheimnisvollem Trieb
Die Kräfte der Natur rings um mich her enthüllen."

440 f.: "Ich schau' in diesen reinen Zügen
Die wirkende Natur vor meiner Seele liegen."

455 ff.: "Wo fass' ich dich, unendliche Natur?
Euch Brüste, wo? Ihr Quellen alles Lebens,
An denen Himmel und Erde hängt. . . ."

For this turning from book learning to the magical apprehension of the book of nature, as illustrated in Cusanus and one group of his Renaissance successors, see Cassirer, *Individuum*, 53, n. 1, and 57 f.

3. Johann Jacob Brucker, *Erste Anfangsgründe der philosophischen Geschichte*, 2nd ed., Ulm, 1751; Daniel Georg Morhof, *Polyhistor, Literarius, Philosophicus et Practicus*, 4th ed., 2 vols., Lübeck, 1747 (see esp. I, 398 f. and II, 246ff.). The former is probably what Goethe referred to in *Dichtung und Wahrheit* as "der kleine Brucker" (*W.A.* I, 27, 12), though he may possibly have meant *Auszug aus den kurtzen Fragen . . .* , Ulm, 1736. Bart-

scherer, *Paracelsus*, e.g. 123, refers to his *Kurtze Fragen aus der philosophischen Historie*, 7 vols., Ulm, 1731-36, and supplement, 1737, as "der kleine Brucker"; it is actually "der grosse Brucker," out of which grew his famous Latin *Historia Critica Philosophiae*. Young Goethe did, however, have easy access to the large Brucker since it was in his father's library.

4. Robert Petsch commentary, 645, note to lines 1126 ff., with references to Balthasar Bekker and the Faust book. Witkowski (II, 208) gives an equally general reference from Johann Praetorius, *Anthropodemus Plutonicus*, with vague citing of "other works." Agnes Bartscherer (Paracelsus, 123 f.) found a summary of Fludd's exposition in Brucker, though she was not led thereby to consult Fludd's work itself with its vivid engravings.

5. For what is probably the most comprehensive account see Rudolf Allers, "Microcosmus from Anaximandros to Paracelsus," *Traditio*, II (1944), 319-407. Unfortunately, I did not read this notable work until just before the final revisions of this study, but I have incorporated its results at several points, as the notes indicate. I have not seen G. P. Conger, *Theories of Macrocosms and Microcosms in the History of Philosophy*, New York, 1922. See also the brief, meaty account in Arnold, esp. 240, for the important place which the concept held in the Stoic philosophy.

6. The *Tabula Smaragdina* of Hermes Trismegistus is to be found in countless Renaissance and later books, usually in Latin, though often in German and other modern languages. See the monograph by Julius Ruska, *Tabula Smaragdina*, Heidelberg, 1926. The standard edition of the *Poemander*, Gustav Parthey ed., Berlin, 1854, does not include the *Tabula*, but the German translation by Alethophilus (numerous ed. from 1706 onward, repr. Stuttgart, 1855) does contain it in the introduction (repr., 51 f.). The latest edition and most comprehensive study of the corpus of writings ascribed to Hermes Trismegistus is Walter Scott's *Hermetica*, 4 vols., Oxford, 1924-36. In young Goethe's letter to Ernst Theodor Langer, April 29, 1770 (*Goethes Briefe an E. Th. Langer*, Paul Zimmermann ed., Wolfenbüttel, 1922, p. 28; not in *W.A.*) the "Faustian" setting of his reference to Hermes is noteworthy.

7. See 1. *The New Schaff-Herzog Encyclopedia of Religious Knowledge*, Samuel Macauley Jackson ed., New York and London, 1910, article "Mani, Manicheans," pt. 11: "When one of the adepts dies and his soul leaves his body, the original man sends a

light-god in the form of a wise guide, i.e. Jesus, and with him three other light-deities and a light-maiden, who carry five articles which symbolize relationship to the kingdom of light—a water vessel, a cloak, a head-band, a crown, and a wreath of light. . . . The symbolic articles are received by the soul, which then ascends to the moon. . . ." 2. Francis Crawford Burkitt, *The Religion of the Manichees*, Cambridge, 1925, 43: ". . . the Description of Manichaeism in the Acts of Archelaus (c. viii) . . . tells us that when Jesus was sent on His message of salvation He contrived a vast mechanism, like a water-wheel with twelve buckets, which takes up the souls of men and the light-particles in their bodies as they die to the Moon, which thus waxes for fifteen days. While in the Moon the souls are somehow purged and purified by the Sun, and then the Moon empties itself of the purged Light, whereby it wanes for another fifteen days."

Heinrich Düntzer in his *Faust* commentary (2 vols., Leipzig, 1850, I, 174) seems to have been the first to suggest Manichaean origins for Goethe's image. Burdach developed this most elaborately (and unconvincingly) into the picture of an irrigation wheel in an oriental oasis-garden with ministering attendants; see his *Faust und Moses*, 763-766 and notes.

8. See e.g. Benjamin Bickley Rogers ed. and tr., ΑΡΙΣΤΟΦΑΝΤΣ ΚΩΜΩΙΔΙΑΙ *The Comedies of Aristophanes*, vol. II, London, 1916, 38 and 39, ΝΕΦΕΛΑΙ (*The Clouds*), line 272 (Socrates' invocation to the clouds):

εἴτ ἄρα Νείλου προχοαῖς ὑδάτων χρυσέαις ἀρύεσθε προχοῖσιν

"Or stoop to enfold with your pitchers of gold, the mystical waves of the Nile."

(more literally: "whether you be drawing up the waves of the Nile in golden urns.")

9. Lines 359-365. The German translation of 364-365 by Johann Jacob Bodmer, 3rd rev. ed., 2 vols., Zürich, 1754, reads (II, 21 f.): "Andere Sternen schöpfen hier in ihren güldenen Krügen das Licht, so sie nöthig haben, als aus ihrem Brunnen." Thomas Keightley in his edition of Milton (2 vols., London, 1859, II, 19 note) says: "Milton was probably indebted for this beautiful image to the Scholiast on Euripides, *Phoen.* 175."

10. Lines 423-424; continues: "In humid exhalations, and at even Sups with the ocean." This comes from the Stoic natural philosophy of Cleanthes and Posidonius by way of Macrobius' *Saturnalia* I, 23, 2; see Arnold, 184 and n. 69. Compare Goethe's earth-

centered variant of this notion, in Biedermann III, 368 f., in a remarkably pertinent setting (Earth Spirit, the Cusanian principles of knowledge, etc.).

11. See notes 9 and 10 above; also Cicero, *De Natura Deorum*, H. Rackham ed. and tr., London and New York, 1933, 161-163 and 235 (i.e. Book II, ch. xv and xlvi), the latter especially important for emphasizing the cyclic nature of the transfer of matter and energy: "But the stars are of a fiery substance, and for this reason they are nourished by the vapours of the earth, the sea and the waters, which are raised up by the sun out of the fields which it warms and out of the waters; and when nourished and renewed by these vapours the stars and the whole aether shed them back again, and then once more draw them up from the same source. . . ." The cyclic transmutation of the four kinds of matter (the four elements) by successive condensation and rarefaction, and their oneness with spirit (aether, light, celestial fire) is also basic Stoic doctrine (e.g. *ibid.*, 203-205; Book II, ch. xxxiii), and came down to Fludd, Milton, and others. It is, of course, in direct opposition to Platonic and Neoplatonic dualism, which exalts the spiritual and debases the material. Cf. Ovid, *Metamorphoses*, xv, 237-251.

12. For a convenient and accessible summary see Kienast (above ch. II, n. 18), 100-105, 108, and commentary 117 (n. 5), 123 (n. 21), 124 (n. 24).

13. *Les Prophéties de M. Michel Nostradamus*, first ed., Lyon, 1555, first complete ed., Lyon, 1568 (for bibliographical details see Carl von Klinckowstroem, "Die ältesten Ausgaben der 'Prophéties' des Nostradamus," *Zeitschrift für Bücherfreunde*, n.s. IV, 1912/13, 361-372). The edition by Theophilus de Garencières, *The True Prophecies or Prognostications of Michael Nostradamus*, London, 1672, used for this study, contains the original French quatrains, as well as the English translation and the extensive commentary of the editor. See esp. p. 1-4, and the preface, leaf e (1, r-v). The French original of the two first quatrains reads:

> "Estant assis, de nuit secrette estude,
> Seul, reposé sur la selle d'airain,
> Flambe exigüe, sortant de solitude,
> Fait proferer qui n'est a croire vain.

> "La Verge en main, mise au milieu des Branches,
> De l'Onde je moüille & le Limbe & le Pied,

En peur j'escris fremissant par les manches;
Splendeur Divine: le Divine prez s'assied."

Garencières follows Servius' commentaries on Virgil in explaining the brazen stool as a table (tablet) set upon a tripod.

One attempt to explain Goethe's reference as being so meant was Robert Petsch's "Nostradamus im Faust," *Wissenschaftliches Korrespondenzblatt der Philologiae Novitates,* October, 1906, 4-6. I have not seen this short study, but according to the review in the *Jahresberichte für neuere deutsche Literaturgeschichte,* 17-18 (1906-07), 873, Petsch based his article on Morhof's *Polyhistor,* citing passages from it on Nostradamus' prophecies, "Aber von alledem ist eben gar nichts in die Faustdichtung übergegangen, und so schwebt P.s Darlegung gänzlich in der Luft." See also the Petsch commentary, 638, where the emphasis is still on astrology. See also Bartscherer, *Zur Kenntnis,* 31-40, which comes closer to the elucidation of Goethe's probable intent than any subsequent commentary.

Considering the numerous editions of Nostradamus' book and the relatively large number of copies that have survived, it seems more likely than not that a young man of Goethe's proclivities and interests would have had access to a copy of the book and would have examined it with considerable interest. Indeed, it could only be by some strange accident that he would have failed to do so.

See also Wieland's interesting allusion to Nostradamus in the whimsical tribute to young Goethe contained in the poem, "An Psychen," *Wielands Werke,* vol. XII, Wilhelm Kurrelmeyer ed., Berlin, 1935, 76:

"Doch wenig half izt ihm und mir
Sein *Nostradamus!* Er konnt', ums Leben,
Nur nicht den Pferden Flügel geben!
Da sassen wir grosse Geister, wir!"

Even this light jest will serve to indicate what connotations the name Nostradamus readily summoned up in the Weimar circle of 1775. On closer scrutiny the poem offers several interesting suggestions which deserve to be followed up.

14. Paul Oskar Kristeller, *The Philosophy of Marsilio Ficino,* New York, 1943, 309-313, esp. 312. That such thoughts of transcendence of time were familiar to Goethe is indicated with ample reference in Franz Koch, "Fausts Gang zu den Müttern," *Fest-*

schrift der Nationalbibliothek in Wien, Wien, 1926, 509-528; p. 519 and notes. Page 516 contains a welcome demonstration of the relation of the scene about the Mothers to trains of thought from Goethe's youth, though Koch had no inkling of any connection from the Nostradamus allusion in the first monologue to this scene. See also the section, "Vergangenheit und Gegenwart," in his *Goethes Stellung zu Tod und Unsterblichkeit,* Schriften der Goethe-Gesellschaft, 45 (1932), esp. 158 ff., with its rich collection of illustrative material from Goethe's works, though almost no attempt is made to trace the sources and origins of this mode of thought in Goethe. I have not seen Koch's separate paper on the subject, "Vergangenheit und Gegenwart in eins," *Freies deutsches Hochstift, Frankfurt a. M., Reihe der Vorträge und Schriften,* vol. 1, Halle, 1939.

15. *W.A.* 1, 39, 201:

"Weil ich glaubte
Sie sähen das Vergangene, das Zukünftige
Im Gegenwärtigen."

16. *W.A.* iv, 3, 51 f.:
"Ich kann mir die Bedeutsamkeit—die Macht, die diese Frau über mich hat, anders nicht erklären, als durch die Seelenwanderung.—Ja, wir waren einst Mann und Weib!—Nun wissen wir von uns—verhüllt, in Geisterduft.—Ich habe keine Namen für uns—die Vergangenheit—die Zukunft—das All."

W.A. 1, 4, 97:

"Warum gabst du uns die tiefen Blicke,
Unsre Zukunft ahnungsvoll zu schaun,

. . .

Ach du warst in abgelebten Zeiten
Meine Schwester oder meine Frau."

17. *W.A.* 1, 38, 16: "Wir gingen neulich, mein Gemahl und ich, in dem Hain jenseits des Cocytus, wo, wie du weisst, die Gestalten der Träume sich lebhaft darstellen und hören lassen."

18. *W.A.* 1, 28, 284 (also the following pages): "Ein Gefühl aber, das bei mir gewaltig überhand nahm und sich nicht wundersam genug äussern konnte, war die Empfindung der Vergangenheit und Gegenwart in Eins: eine Anschauung, die etwas Gespenstermässiges in die Gegenwart brachte. Sie ist in vielen meiner grössern und kleinern Arbeiten ausgedrückt und wirkt im Ge-

dicht immer wohltätig, ob sie gleich im Augenblick, wo sie sich unmittelbar am Leben und im Leben selbst ausdrückte, jedermann seltsam, unerklärlich, vielleicht unerfreulich scheinen musste. "Köln war der Ort, wo das Altertum eine solche unzuberechnende Wirkung auf mich ausüben konnte." See also Biedermann II, 173.

19. See Cassirer, *Individuum*, 186-190 (epitomized in Allers, 382); also his "Pico," 323 and 337. *Faust*, lines 6214, 6222 f., 6275 f.:

"Um sie kein Ort, noch weniger eine Zeit . . ."
". . . Kein Weg! Ins Unbetretene,
Nicht zu Betretende . . ."
"Versinke denn! Ich könnt' auch sagen: steige!
's ist einerlei."

20. Biedermann IV, 184 (Dec. 20, 1829): ". . . er ist darin den Gespenstern ähnlich, die überall gegenwärtig sein und zu jeder Stunde hervortreten können."

21. *W.A.* IV, 42, 197 f.: ". . . nun mag sie im Zeitmoment solidesziert endlich verharren."

22. See e.g. Gräf, 400 f. and 432; i.e. Biedermann III, 407 f. (July 5, 1827), and *W.A.* IV, 43, 266 f. (letter to Karl Friedrich von Reinhard, Jan. 28, 1828).

23. See e.g. Arnold, 112. Goethe used the image of mother and suckling child with larger symbolic intent in his early poems, "Der Wanderer" and "Künstlers Morgenlied," in the latter with startling pagan accretions which are not willfully subjective but solidly traditional (*W.A.* I, 2, 170 and 180).

VI. THE EARTH SPIRIT

1. See above ch. V, n. 13.

2. Typically summarized by Witkowski II, 195. The passages are lines 460-517, 1744-47, 3217-46, and in the prose scene "Trüber Tag."

3. *W.A.* I, 37, 188: "Die Fülle der heiligsten tiefsten Empfindung drängte für einen Augenblick den Menschen zum überirdischen Wesen, er redete die Sprache der Geister, und aus den Tiefen der Gottheit flammte seine Zunge Leben und Licht. Auf der Höhe der Empfindung erhält sich kein Sterblicher. Und

doch musste den Jüngern die Erinnerung jenes Augenblicks Wonne durch ein ganzes Leben nachvibrieren. Wer fühlt nicht in seinem Busen, dass er sich unaufhörlich wieder dahin sehnen würde?"

4. Carl Roos, "Zur 'Quellen'-Frage der Erdgeistszene und zur Spinoza-Frage," *Jahrbuch der Goethe-Gesellschaft*, XVI (1930), 183-208; and cf. Burdach, "Das religiöse Problem," 78 f.

5. Witkowski II, 195, and plates 5 and 7 (p. 469 and 471).

6. *W.A.* IV, 31, 163 f., to Carl Friedrich Moritz Paul, Count von Brühl, June 2, 1819.

7. I Corinthians 2, 12; cf. II Corinthians 4, 4, and Romans 8, 15.

8. Witkowski ed. I, 526: "Erscheinung des Geists als Welt und Taten Genius." *Faust*, line 501: "In Lebensfluten, im Tatensturm."

9. See Bartscherer, *Paracelsus*, 94 f.

10. See, e.g. Arnold, 230 f. and 112; also 40, etc.

11. See Allers, 364.

12. *Ibid.*, 349, n. 74.

13. Book IV, lines 219-227:

> "His quidam signis atque haec exempla secuti
> esse apibus partem divinae mentis et haustus
> aetherios dixere; deum namque ire per omnia,
> terrasque tractusque maris caelumque profundum;
> hinc pecudes, armenta, viros, genus omne ferarum,
> quemque sibi tenuis nascentem arcessere vitas;
> scilicet huc reddi deinde ac resoluta referri
> omnia, nec morti esse locum, sed viva volare
> sideris in numerum atque alto succedere caelo."

The English translation is by H. Rushton Fairclough, in his edition of Virgil, 2 vols., London and New York, 1927, I, 211-213. See the commentary by John Conington, ed., *P. Vergili Maronis Opera*, 3 vols., 4th ed., London, 1881, I, 365 and II, 519. Conington cites Heyne on the philosophical interpretation of this and the following passage, and on the resemblance between the latter and Cicero, *De Divinatione* I, ch. 11. But see also Arnold, 80, who finds an important source in the poem of Aratus the Stoic, the *Phaenomena*.

14. Fairclough ed. I, 557. The original passage, Book VI, lines 726-731 (I add also the two preceding lines):

> "Principio caelum ac terras camposque liquentis
> lucentemque globum lunae Titaniaque astra

spiritus intus alit, totamque infusa per artus
mens agitat molem et magno se corpore miscet.
inde hominum pecudumque genus, vitaeque volantum,
et quae marmoreo fert monstra sub aequore pontus.
igneus est ollis vigor et caelestis origo
seminibus. . . ."

15. Ovid, *Metamorphoses*, Book xv, line 165; translation by
Frank Justus Miller, 2 vols., London and New York, 1926, II, 377,
389, 377 and 383. Latin originals.
Lines 342-345:

"Nam sive est animal tellus et vivit habetque
spiramenta locis flammam exhalantia multis,
spirandi mutare vias, quotiensque movetur,
has finire potest, illas aperire cavernas."

Lines 181-184:

"sed ut unda inpellitur unda
urgueturque eadem veniens urguetque priorem,
tempora sic fugiunt pariter pariterque sequuntur
et nova sunt semper."

Lines 255-257:

"nascique vocatur
incipere esse aliud, quam quod fuit ante, morique
desinere illud idem."

16. *W.A.* I, 27, 319 f.
17. Book II, ch. 4; *W.A.* I, 24, 307.
18. *W.A.* I, 37, 98-99 (see also above ch. I, n. 21). Of Goethe's
four entries from *De Divinatione*, the first is of considerable significance in this connection: "Cumque omnia completa et referta
sint aeterno sensu, et mente divina, necesse est cognatione [recte:
contagione] divinorum animorum, animos humanos commoveri."
(Book I, ch. XLIX; see also ch. LI, LVI and LVII, esp. in relation to
the discussion of Nostradamus.)
19. Ch. II. The English translation is by William Armistead
Falconer, in Cicero, *De Senectute, De Amicitia, De Divinatione*,
London and New York, 1927, 243-245. The Latin text:

"principio aetherio flammatus Iuppiter igni
vertitur et totum conlustrat lumine mundum,

menteque divina caelum terrasque petessit,
quae penitus sensus hominum vitasque retentat
aetheris aeterni saepta atque inclusa cavernis.
Et, si stellarum motus cursusque vagantis
nosse velis, . . .
omnia iam cernes divina mente notata.

. . .

cum claram speciem concreto lumine luna
abdidit et subito stellanti nocte perempta est.

. . .

aut cum se gravido tremefecit corpore tellus."

It should be noted that the words "divina mente," the divine spirit
suffused through the world and animating it, are used twice, the
first time very specifically with reference to Jupiter, the second
time inferentially so. It should also be noted that the scope of
reference to the passage in *Faust*, and to Goethe's general concept,
is strictly limited to a few though significant traits.

20. See A. O. Prickard, ed. and tr., *Selected Essays of Plutarch*,
Oxford, 1918, II, 272 ("Of the Face which appears on the Orb of
the Moon," section XII). See also above ch. II, n. 12.

21. Quoted by Pierre Bayle (*The Dictionary*, English translation, London, 1738, v, 199): "Albertus, in I. Phys. *Tract. iii, cap.
xiii*, apud Pererium de communibus Principiis, *lib. v, cap. xii,
pag. m.* 309, 310." Latin text: "Alexander Epicureus dixit Deum
esse materiam, vel non esse extra ipsam, & omnia essentialiter esse
Deum, & formas esse accidentia imaginata; & non habere veram
entitatem, & ideo dixit omnia idem esse substantialiter, & hunc
Deum appellavit aliquando Jovem, aliquando Apollinem, & aliquando Palladem; & formas esse peplum Palladis, & vestem Jovis;
& neminem sapientum ajebat ad plenum revelare posse ea quae
latebant sub peplo Palladis & sub veste Jovis." Quoted in part,
without indication of omissions, by Witkowski II, 196; the omitted
portions are essential toward understanding the larger scope of
reference of this passage to Goethe's Macrocosm and Earth Spirit.
This Alexander Epicureus has never been identified, though Bayle
offers some conjectures; among the hundred odd Alexanders
listed in the Pauly-Wissowa, *Real-Encyclopädie der classischen
Altertumswissenschaft*, there is not one with whom he could be
identified. The passage could hardly be Epicurean; it is probably
Stoic, possibly transmitted by an eclectic philosopher.

It is to be noted as a parallel that in the eighth Orphic Hymn Helios is equated with Zeus, in the eleventh Pan with Zeus, and in the thirty-fourth Apollo with Pan. Proteanism in unity is one of the characteristic features of these mystical invocations, and their effect on Goethe's poetic symbolism still needs to be studied. He tells us in his autobiography that the three manifestations of Greek thought toward which he felt the greatest sympathy in early youth were Hesiod, the Orphic poems, and the Stoic philosophy (*W.A.* I, 27, 11 f.) On Robert Fludd's statement that the Cabalists also believed that we find God in nature clad in multiple vestments, see Denis Saurat, *Milton et le matérialisme Chrétien en Angleterre*, Paris, 1928, p. 20.

22. Plutarch's essay, "On the 'E' at Delphi," Prickard transl. II, 67. This passage (section IX) on divine proteanism is especially important. The concept of the divinity of matter, the truth of phenomena, the world as the garment of God, goes from Zeno, through Posidonius, to Philo, and so to the *Zohar*. In the Renaissance this influence from the *Cabala* fortified the direct transmission through Cicero and others, when Pico, Reuchlin, and their followers took up their Cabalistic studies. Denis Saurat traces the tradition into the Renaissance exclusively via the *Zohar*, without mentioning its Stoic origins and its more direct transmission, but he performs that task very ably, and demonstrates how antagonistic all this was to Neoplatonic concepts. See esp. his *Literature and Occult Tradition*, tr. Dorothy Bolton, New York, 1930, p. 64 *et passim*, and his *Milton, Man and Thinker*, New York, 1925, p. 280 note, and 281-300.

23. Benedict Figulus ed., *Pandora Magnalium Naturalium*, Strassburg, 1608, p. 1-16. This tract, as no one previously has noticed, was first published in London, 1566, by Giovanni Battista Agnello with his commentary. Then it appeared in the folio ed. of Paracelsus' works, vol. II, Strassburg, 1603, then in the *Alchimia Vera*, n.p., 1604 (see n. 25 below). Bartscherer (*Paracelsus*, 89 ff. and *Zur Kenntnis*, 31) treats it as though it were a genuine work of Paracelsus, but her exposition is highly interesting and worthy of consideration. Karl Sudhoff (*Versuch einer Kritik der Echtheit der Paracelsischen Schriften*, 3 parts in 2 vols., Berlin, 1894-99, nos. 257, 265, 282, 508), though not aware of its provenience, rightly excludes it from the Paracelsus canon. The tract was reprinted in 1771 (no. 462) and was thus easily available to young Goethe, here as well as in the works of Paracelsus.

P. 4: "Dieser Geist wirdt von Avicenna genandt die Seel der Welt. Dann gleich wie die Seel alle Glieder des Leibs beweget: Also beweget dieser Geist alle Cörper/ Vnd wie die Seele in allen Gliedern des Leibs ist: Also findet sich dieser Geist in allen Elementirten Geschöpffen."

P. 9-10: "Dieser Geist ist das Geheimnuss/ das von anbegin ist verborgen gewesen . . . welcher Fewrig in der lufft wohnet/ vnd das Erdreich mit jhm gehn Himmel führet. . . . Dieser Geist fleugt durch das mittel der Himmel/ wie ein Aussgehēder Morgengewölck/ führet sein Brennend Fewer im Wasser/ vnd hat sein Clarificirtes Erdrich im Himmel."

"Derohalben soltu dich mit diesem Geist nicht einlassen/ Du verstehests dann genugsamlich."

P. 11: "Diese Geistliche Substantz ist weder Himlich noch Hellisch: Sondern ein lufftiges reines/ vnd herrliches Corpus, vnnd das gestalte mittel Zwischen dem Höchsten vnnd vntersten. . . ."

24. Lines 468-474:

> "Es wölkt sich über mir—
> Der Mond verbirgt sein Licht—
> Die Lampe schwindet!
> Es dampft!—Es zucken rote Strahlen
> Mir um das Haupt—Es weht
> Ein Schauer vom Gewölb' herab
> Und fasst mich an!"

25. In the *Alchimia Vera*, ed., J.P.S.M.S., n.p., 1604 (another ed., n.d., prob. 1611, in the Winthrop library, and apparently one or two further slightly variant editions). As stated in note 23 above, this collection also includes the "Apocalypse of the Secret Spirit of the World," under a variant title. The "Colloquium" is reprinted in Will-Erich Peuckert, *Pansophie Ein Versuch zur Geschichte der weissen und schwarzen Magie*, Stuttgart, 1936, 557-561. Peuckert makes no reference to its analogies to Goethe's *Faust*, though from other, indirect references of his, in this volume and in other writings, it would seem that he has long since sensed the broader Renaissance implications of the drama. Perhaps he was reserved here because of what he, and Sudhoff before him, considered to be the excessive rarity of the *Alchimia Vera*. But I find that it was not nearly so rare; the dialogue itself was otherwise reprinted, one such reprint (or rather variant version) being

in my personal library (appended to Michael Sendivogius, *Tripvs Chimicvs*, Strassburg, 1628; the dialogue here is dated Feb. 18, 1568, instead of Feb. 2, 1560).

Excerpts from the "Colloqvivm Spiritvs Mercvrij et Monachi, Fratris Alberti Beyeri, Ordinis Carmelitarum":

"Spiritus: Was ist die vrsache/ das du mich mit so viel Abgöttischen Abergläubischen Coniurationibus Zauberungen gebannet hast? . . .

"Ich bin weder ein guter noch böser Engel/ sondern bin einer aus den sieben Planeten-Geistern/ die da beherrschen die mittel Natur/ denen befohlen ist zu regieren die vier vnterschiedliche Theil der gantzen Welt/ nemblich/ das Firmamentische/ Animalische/ Vegetabilische vnd Mineralische theil. . . .

"Ich heisse vnnd bin der Geist dess Planeten vnd nicht dess Gottes Mercurij/ wie du jhnen inn deinen Incantationibus Coniurationibus nicht hast zu dir bracht/ Sondern bin durch Gottes zulassung/ gantz freywillig vngezwungen zu dir kommen/ derenthalben mich auch dein Circkel/ Liechter vnd Schwerdt/ auch die andern Fantasey weniger denn nichts angehet. . . .

"Ich Frater Albertus Beyer . . . bezeuge hiemit . . . das Anno salutis 1560 den 2. Februarij . . . mir . . . ein solches Gesicht erschienen/ vnd vorgemeldtes Colloquium mit mir gehalten/ nach dem ich Tag vnnd Nacht mit Philosophischen Büchern auffstund vnd zu Bette gieng/ vnd Gott den HErren mit embsiglichen seufftzen Tag vnd Nacht bat/ das er mir die warheit dieser Kunst gnediglichen offenbaren wolte/ da habe ich in meiner vnwissenheit/ Gott vorzeihe mir es/ weil ich anderst nicht vormeint/ nach dem ich 23. Jhar mit meinem Apte vergeblich mit grosser mühe laborirt/ vnd das Fewer vmb sonst gemartert/ man köndte das hohe Geheimniss von keinem Menschen lernen/ sondern man müste es von Geistern erzwingen/ da es doch der Menschen viel mehr ist als den Geistern. . . . Da sage ich/ habe auff bemeldem tag durch gewönlich Ceremonien vnd gebreuchliche Coniurationes . . . den Spiritum Mercurij beschworen/ vnd auff ein Gespräch gefordert. . . ."

26. See above ch. V, n. 6; the first dialogue, properly called the *Poemander* (Ποιμάνδρης), after which the whole collection of fourteen (or more) pieces is usually named.

27. The new edition of the works of Kepler (Max Caspar, gen. ed.), München, 1937 ff. has not been completed and was not available to me, nor were Caspar's German translations of several

works, nor was his biography, unfortunately. My references are to the old edition of the *Opera Omnia*, Christian Frisch ed., 8 vols., Frankfurt & Erlangen, 1858-70. The *Harmonices* references: v, 250-267 (esp. 251 and 253-257), also 326 and 327. The *Epitome* references: vi, esp. 176-179. Kepler's statements on various relevant themes: the Mothers, the concept of polarity, man's fate and freedom, must be left for another occasion.

28. Frisch ed. ii, 270 f.; Prickard transl. ii, 274 f.

29. Frisch ed. v, 61 and 63 f.

30. *Ibid.* vii, 29 f., in the tract, *Ausführlicher Bericht von dem newlich . . . erschienenen Haarstern oder Cometen*, Halle, 1608. Plutarch's "On the Cessation of the Oracles" seems to have been a point of departure, though Kepler's development goes its own way.

31. *Ibid.* i, 542, at the conclusion of the tract, *Antwort Joannis Keppleri . . . auff D. Helisaei Röslini . . . Discours Von heutiger zeit beschaffenheit*, Prag, 1609: "*Kepplerus*: . . . Aber meine oben gesetzte argumenta bringen zum ersten eine Seel in den Erdboden, die den principatum huius actionis vber jren Leib, nemblich vber die kugel habe. . . . *D. Röslin*: Diser spiritus muss mir aber durch die gantze Welt gehen vnd nit der Erden aigen, sondern von geburt aetherius sein. *Keppler*: Ich lass ein sollichen algemeinen spiritum auch in meim Buch passieren: aber darneben hab ich für die Erdkugel ein eignen, vnd beweiss jhne auss jetzerzehlten vnd mehrern seinen verrichtungen."

32. *Ibid.* v, 326 and 327: ". . . in Sole vero intellectum simplicem, πυρ νοερον σευ νουν habitare, omnis harmoniae fontem, quicunque ille sit." "An non vel sensus ipsi exclamant, ignea hic habitare corpora, mentium simplicium capacia, vereque Solem esse πυρος νοερον si non regem, at saltem regiam?"

33. W. Carl Rufus, "Kepler as an Astronomer," in *Johann Kepler 1571-1630 A Tercentenary Commemoration of his Life and Work*, Baltimore, 1931, p. 36. The editor, Frederick E. Brasch, has appended an excellent "Bibliography of the Works of Johann Kepler" to the volume, 86-133. In contrast to the other essays, the one by E. H. Johnson, "Kepler and Mysticism," is virtually nineteenth century in attitude, and misses the point.

34. *Ibid.*, p. xi f.

35. Cf. note 27 above; Ludwig Günther, ed. and tr., *Traum oder nachgelassenes Werk über die Astronomie des Mondes*, Leipzig, 1898; Otto J. Bryk, ed. and tr. (selec.), *Die Zusammen-*

klänge der Welten, Jena, 1918; Max Caspar, ed. and tr., *Neue Astronomie*, München, Berlin, 1929, *Das Weltgeheimnis, Mysterium Cosmographicum*, 1936, *Weltharmonik*, 1939, and *Johannes Kepler in seinen Briefen* (ed. with Walther von Dyck), 1930.
36. See esp. Marjorie Hope Nicolson, "Cosmic Voyages," *ELH A Journal of English Literary History*, vii (1940), 83-107; "Kepler, the *Somnium*, and John Donne," *Journal of the History of Ideas*, i (1940), 259-280; and *Voyages to the Moon*, New York, 1948.

VII. THE EASTER WALK AND BEYOND

1. See ch. VI, n. 23; *Pandora*, p. 50: "Aber Ich sehe dass die guten Herren noch im Buchstaben stecken/ wie Ich auch darauff viel gehaltē."
P. 54: "die Bawren so sie frassen/ sturben/ Erkrümbten vnd Erlahmbten . . . du warest noch ein Junger Medicus, die Praxis liess sich so bald nicht lernen/ solst dich darinnen vben/ die Leuht weidlich tödten vnd hinrichten/ so würdestu einen rechten Medicum geben."
(*Faust*, lines 1057-59:

"Tut nicht ein braver Mann genug,
Die Kunst, die man ihm übertrug,
Gewissenhaft und pünktlich auszuüben?")

P. 58: "Ich bin auch selbst darbey gewesen/ da ein Junger Fürst kranck war/ uñ sie nicht wusten/ wo hinauss/ da sprach einer/ Procedamus secundum Methodum & erimus excusati, wie gefellt dir dieser Rath/ Ewer Methodus muss gelten/ vnd solten Alle Fürsten dē Geist drob auffgeben."
P. 64: "Die Scientia ist vber Menschlichen Verstand/ Eine Gabe vnd ein Wunderwerck Gottes: der mit Menschlichen verstand dieselben vermeinet Zuergreiffen/ Der Irret/ ohne Offenbarung dess H. Geistes/ vnd eingebung Gottes/ wirdt sie Niemand bekommen. Es sey Baccalaureus, Meyster/ oder Doctor. Vnser Künst auss den Hohen Schulen helffen Vns nicht zu diesem Geheimniss."
P. 65 f.: ". . . der Buchstaben ist ein vrsach aller jrrung/ vnd Niemand wills mercken das der Buchstab tod ist."
P. 99: "Paracelsus hat keinen grössern Feind/ dann die Galenischen Medicos, die vberreden sich/ wañ sie vber ein Buch kommen/ dasselbige lesen/ wissen sie schon/ was es sagt. Aber die

Hochgelehrten dölpel betrachten nicht/ dass Paracelsus seine Bücher Stylo Magyco beschrieben. So ist auch ihr hirn voller Witz/ dass Intellectus Magicus nicht hinein kan. Darumb schreyen sie/ Magia ist Zauberey/ hütet euch/ es ist Teuffels werck/ da doch Magia keine Zauberey/ sondern die aller gröste Weissheit Göttlicher werck ist/ vnnd eine erkenner in [i.e., erkennerin] verborgener Natur."

2. Sign. *vii(v)-viii(v) : "Wann wir aber ... wollen der Wahren Natürlichen Philosophey/ auss dem Liecht der Natur gegründet nachgehen/ vnd dieselbe erlernen/ ... Wo vnd von wem sollen wir sie studiren? Sollen wir deren Doctores vnd Praeceptores bey den Hohen Schulen suchen? Da werden wir sie wahrlich nicht finden. ... Sie wollen lieber bey den Hülsen vnd Sprewern/ die der Wind hin vnnd her verstrewet/ als bey den Edlen wolschmackenden Kern/ Rocken vnd Waitzen auss der Grossen Scheuren oder Schatzkammer dess Ewigen Gottes ... hoc est, Macrocosmo ... verbleiben. Wo sollen wirs dann suchen/ bei welcher Schul frag ich? ... Auss dem Liecht der Natur ... sollen wir lernen ... was auss dem Liecht der Natur ist/ dass muss auss denselbigen erlernet werden. ..."

Sign. ** ij(v)-iij(v) : "Wo müssen wir aber zu vnserm Intent vnd Erforschung der Natur kommen ...? Hinderm offen daheim lernets sich warlich nicht/ vnd wenn wir aller Philosophen Bücher vberm hauffen hetten/ vnd die tag vnd nacht herumb stürmten/ vnnd darauss erlernen wolten/ Nein es thuts nicht: Sondern wann wir die Natur in vnserer Philosophei durchforschen wollen/ vnd zu einem gewünschten glückseligen end gelangen/ so müssen wir d'Natur bücher mit vnsern Füssen treten/ Die Geschrifft erforschet man durch jhren Buchstaben: Die Natur aber durch Land zu Land. ... Da rumb als offt ein Land/ also offt ein Blatt im Buch der Natur zu finden: Also ist nun Codex Naturae satis amplus & largus. Also muss man ihre Bletter mit den Füssen vmbkehren/ vnnd mit dem Geist der vernunfft erforschen. ... Dann alle Creata uñ Geschöpff Gottes sind lebendige Buchstaben vnd Bücher dess Menschen herkommen zubeschreiben: Ja alle Creata sind Buchstaben darinnen gelesen wirdt/ Wer der Mensch ist. ..."

Sign. **iij(v)-iv(v) : "Darumb begnüget mir billich an diesen Dreyen Büchern/ darauss ich alle Weissheit schöpffen vnnd erlernen möge: Als an dem grossen mächtigen Circkelrundē Buch der Natur/ so nit mit dinten/ oder Stylo geschrieben/ sondern

mit dem Finger Gottes . . . : Welches Buch Macrocosmus genennet wirdt. Zum Andern An dem kleinē Buch/ welches mit
allen seinen Blettern vnd Stücken auss dem grossen genommen/
vnnd darnach formirt ist worden/ Welches der Mensch ist . . .
vnd dieses wird Microcosmus genennet: Vnd ist der Mensch
allein Der/ Der ein Instrument ist dess Natürlichē Liechts/ das
jehnig zuvolbringen/ dieselbigen werck in Künsten vnd Weissheit darzu thun/ wie sie dann Gott im Firmament verordnet hat.
Also hat er auch weitters verordnet/ das der Mensch einen zwey-
fachen Magneten habe/ Einen Nemlich von den Elementen/
darumb zeucht er sie widerumb an sich: Darnach einen auss dem
Gestirn/ auss dem er an sich Zeucht die Microcosmische Siñlig-
keit widerumb vom Gestirn/ vnnd hat also die Vernunfft dess
Menschen einen Magneten/ der in sich Zeucht vom Gestirn die
Sinn vnd Gedancken. . . . Darumb ist auch wol zumercken/ das
zwo Sehlen im Menschen sind/ die Ewig vnd die Natürlich/
das ist zwey Leben: Eins ist dem Todt vnderworffen/ Das Ander
widerstehet dem Todt: Also auch die zwen-Geist/ der Ewig vnd
der Natürlich. . . ."
　Sign. ** v(r): "Das Dritte Buch ist Nemblich Sacra Biblia, die
H. Hochwürdige Schrifft Alt vnd New Testaments das weiset
vns auff diese 2. vorgehende Bücher hinein. . . ."
　3. See, e.g. Arnold, 57 and 69 f. Allers (358 n. 101, 365 and 366
n. 127 and 129) treats the speculative tradition about the two souls
one-sidedly, from the point of view of good-evil dualism. On
the other hand, Witkowski (commentary to lines 1110-17 and
11958-65) gives, on the whole, a well-balanced and judicious account of what must have been Goethe's intent here. On Pico's
exposition of the two souls, the strife on earth, and the resolution
in heaven in "the embraces of our blessed mother," see his "Oration," sec. 12-14 (op. cit., 230 f.).
　4. Lines 11958-65:

> "Wenn starke Geisteskraft
> Die Elemente
> An sich herangerafft,
> Kein Engel trennte
> Geeinte Zwienatur
> Der innigen beiden,
> Die ewige Liebe nur
> Vermag's zu scheiden."

Cf., e.g. Plutarch, "Of the Face . . . ," sec. xxviii (Prickard transl. ii, 303 f.). On the Manichaean parallels see above ch. V, n. 7. See also Allers, 364, n. 120.

5. Arnold, 206; see also 207 f. and esp. 330. Perhaps the earliest poetic expression of this conviction that has survived occurs in Cleanthes' beautiful "Hymn to Zeus" (*ibid.*, 86): "For ill and good thy power doth so combine that out of all appears in unity Eternal Reason." In the Renaissance one of the most outspoken upholders of this old Stoic (and Cabalistic) doctrine that evil is part of God's plan and that the material proceeds from God and is his creative consort, was Leone Ebreo, in his *Dialoghi d'Amore*; see Robb, esp. 210 f., also 197-203.

6. Robb, 67 f. and 87; cf. 83, also 116 f. and 133 f. Cusanus even declares that the human spirit can awaken to true life only in contact with the world of senses. The spirit is the seed, the potentiality, which can develop to full self-realization only in the soil of the material. See Cassirer, *Individuum*, 47 f. and notes; also 140 f. on Ficino's exposition of this reciprocal relation, and 142 on its connection with the dual nature of the artist. One of Goethe's strongest expressions of this point of view occurs in his little essay, "Bedeutende Fördernis durch ein einziges geistreiches Wort" (*W.A.* ii, 11, 59): "Hiebei bekenn ich, dass mir von jeher die grosse und so bedeutend klingende Aufgabe: 'Erkenne dich selbst!' immer verdächtig vorkam, als eine List geheim verbündeter Priester, die den Menschen durch unerreichbare Forderungen verwirren und von der Tätigkeit gegen die Aussenwelt zu einer innern falschen Beschaulichkeit verleiten wollten. Der Mensch kennt nur sich selbst, insofern er die Welt kennt, die er nur in sich und sich nur in ihr gewahr wird. Jeder neue Gegenstand, wohl beschaut, schliesst ein neues Organ in uns auf." See also above, ch. I, n. 14.

7. Lines 1110-17:

"Du bist dir nur des einen Triebs bewusst;
O lerne nie den andern kennen!
Zwei Seelen wohnen, ach! in meiner Brust,
Die eine will sich von der andern trennen;
Die eine hält, in derber Liebeslust,
Sich an die Welt mit klammernden Organen;
Die andre hebt gewaltsam sich vom Dust
Zu den Gefilden hoher Ahnen."

8. Lines 304-307:

"Vom Himmel fordert er die schönsten Sterne
Und von der Erde jede höchste Lust,
Und alle Näh' und alle Ferne
Befriedigt nicht die tiefbewegte Brust."

9. Lines 464 f.:

"Ich fühle Mut, mich in die Welt zu wagen,
Der Erde Weh, der Erde Glück zu tragen."

10. Lines 1770-74:

"Und was der ganzen Menschheit zugeteilt ist,
Will ich in meinem innern Selbst geniessen,
Mit meinem Geist das Höchst' und Tiefste greifen,
Ihr Wohl und Weh auf meinen Busen häufen,
Und so mein eigen Selbst zu ihrem Selbst erweitern. . . ."

The lines immediately following in these two passages are:

"Mit Stürmen mich herumzuschlagen
Und in des Schiffbruchs Knirschen nicht zu zagen."

and

"Und, wie sie selbst, am End' auch ich zerscheitern."

11. *W.A.* I, 3, 246 (Zahme Xenien II):

"Und was die Menschen meinen,
Das ist mir einerlei;
Möchte mich mir selbst vereinen,
Allein wir sind zu zwei;
Und im lebendgen Treiben
Sind wir ein Hier und Dort,
Das eine liebt zu bleiben,
Das andre möchte fort;
Doch zu dem Selbstverständnis
Ist auch wohl noch ein Rat:
Nach fröhlichem Erkenntnis
Erfolge rasche Tat."

12. Lines 11441-52:

"Der Erdenkreis ist mir genug bekannt,
Nach drüben ist die Aussicht uns verrannt;
Tor! wer dorthin die Augen blinzelnd richtet,
Sich über Wolken seinesgleichen dichtet!

Er stehe fest und sehe hier sich um;
Dem Tüchtigen ist diese Welt nicht stumm.
Was braucht er in die Ewigkeit zu schweifen!
Was er erkennt, lässt sich ergreifen.
Er wandle so den Erdentag entlang;
Wenn Geister spucken, geh' er seinen Gang,
Im Weiterschreiten find' er Qual und Glück,
Er, unbefriedigt jeden Augenblick!"

This attitude is not only a dramatically appropriate one for Faust to express at this point, it also met with Goethe's personal approval, as he clearly indicated in his statements to Eckermann on April 11, 1827 and April 10, 1829 (Biedermann III, 369, and IV, 104), the former containing a paraphrase of his famous couplet of 1814:

"Willst du ins Unendliche schreiten,
Geh nur im Endlichen nach allen Seiten."

(W.A. I, 2, 216). Very close to Faust's words and possibly a source for them is a passage in the anonymous Latin poem *Aetna*, formerly attributed to Lucilius Junior and even associated with Virgil (lines 252-257):

"sed prior haec hominis cura est cognoscere terram
et quae tot miranda tulit natura notare.
haec nobis magis affinis caelestibus astris.
nam quae mortali spes quaeve amentia maior
in Iovis errantem regno perquirere velle,
tantum opus ante pedes transire et perdere segnem."

See J. Wight Duff and Arnold M. Duff ed., *Minor Latin Poets*, London, 1934, 382 f. English translation: "Yet this is man's more primary task—to know the earth and mark all the many wonders nature has yielded there. This is for us a task more akin than the stars of heaven. For what kind of hope is it for mortal man, what madness could be greater—that he should wish to wander and to explore in Jove's domain and yet pass by the mighty fabric before his feet and lose it in his negligence?" Cf. also lines 224-227.

The *Dicta Catonis* express this attitude with emphatic terseness, book II, no. 2 (*ibid.*, 604 f.):

"An di sint caelumque regant, ne quaere doceri:
cum sis mortalis, quae sunt mortalia cura."

"Ask not if Gods exist or are Heaven's kings:
As thou art mortal, think of mortal things."

13. Lines 1117 f.:

"... Zu den Gefilden hoher Ahnen.
O gibt es Geister in der Luft. ..."

14. For a lucid and adequate summary of the whole philosophical development of the "Logos" concept see Arnold, esp. 35-37, 161 f., and 195 f. Cicero on Zeno, *ibid.* 71 and n. 66; Philo, 23 and 105. See also the articles on the Logos and on Philo Judaeus in the *Encyclopaedia Britannica*, 11th ed. (1911).

15. See lines 1215-37. For this practice see Peuckert, *Pansophie*, 87 f., and esp. Bächtold-Stäubli, *Handwörterbuch des deutschen Aberglaubens*, article "Johannisevangelium." It is only an incidental point that the evil spirits being exorcised howled in pained protest at these words, as did the black poodle.

16. *W.A.* 1, 37, 323 and 325, esp.: "... wie vor jedem grossen *Gedanken der Schöpfung*, wird in der Seele reg was auch Schöpfungskraft in ihr ist." "... dass Schöpfungskraft im Künstler sei aufschwellendes Gefühl der Verhältnisse, Masse und des Gehörigen, und dass nur durch diese ein selbständig Werk, wie andere Geschöpfe durch ihre individuelle Keimkraft hervorgetrieben werden." Here we have the full sequence expressed in "Gedanken," "Kraft," and "Schöpfung" or "Werk." We even have the specific Stoic term "Keimkraft" ("seed-power," "logos spermatikos"). See above ch. V, n. 1.

Ibid., 317: "Jeder Mensch hat mehrmal in seinem Leben die Gewalt dieser Zauberei gefühlt, die den Künstler allgegenwärtig fasst, dadurch ihm die Welt ringsumher belebt wird. ...

"Davon fühlt nun der Künstler nicht allein die Wirkungen, er dringt bis in die Ursachen hinein, die sie hervorbringen. Die Welt liegt vor ihm, möcht ich sagen, wie vor ihrem Schöpfer, der in dem Augenblick, da er sich des Geschaffnen freut, auch alle die Harmonien geniesst, durch die er sie hervorbrachte und in denen sie besteht."

17. Allers, 380 f.; compare with *Faust*, lines 614-620. For Cristoforo Landino's parallel between divine and poetic creation see Robb, 223 and 238: "... And God is the master poet and the world His poem."

The analogy between Divine and human creation is a Stoic commonplace (see e.g. Cicero, *De Natura Deorum*, bk. II, ch. 22

and 34), though its application to the psychology of artistic creation seems first to have developed in the early Renaissance.

18. His "Pico," 341.

19. His *Individuum*, 59: "Und der Prozess der Säkularisierung
vollendet sich, indem weiterhin die Offenbarung des 'Buchs der
Natur' der biblischen Offenbarung gegenübergestellt wird. Zwisch-
en beiden kann kein prinzipieller Gegensatz bestehen, da beide
denselben geistigen Sinn in verschiedener Form darstellen, da
sich in ihnen die Einheit des göttlichen Urhebers der Natur mani-
festiert. Wenn aber trotzdem dem Anschein nach ein solcher
Widerstreit sich für uns auftut, so kann sein Ausgleich nur in
der Weise erfolgen, dass wir der Offenbarung im *Werk* vor der
im *Wort* den Vorzug geben: denn das Wort ist ein Vergangenes
und Überliefertes, während das Werk als Vorhandenes und Dau-
erndes, als ein unmittelbar und gegenwärtig zu Befragendes vor
uns steht."

VIII. CUSANUS AND THE UNITY OF *FAUST*

1. Cassirer, "Pico," esp. 127-131.

2. Cassirer, *Individuum*, esp. 40-48 (note how many further
Goethean-"Faustian" lines of thought are suggested in these
pages); also his "Pico," esp. 137-140.

3. Compare *Faust*, lines 3240-46 (and the second allusion in the
prose scene, "Trüber Tag") with II Corinthians 12, 7: "And lest
I should be exalted above measure through the abundance of the
revelations, there was given to me a thorn in the flesh, the mes-
senger of Satan to buffet me, lest I should be exalted above measure." Oddly enough, this fairly obvious analogue has apparently
been overlooked by the *Faust* commentators, probably as a result
of the biographical explanation which has generally come to be
attached to Paul's words and which consequently has limited its
scope of suggestion.

4. See Cassirer, "Pico," 139 and 325; Robb, 171 f. and 293 f.;
also 36 for Coluccio Salutati's similar convictions and, 35-38, the
dynamic, activistic attitudes that accompany them.

5. Lines 4725-27:

> "*Der* spiegelt ab das menschliche Bestreben.
> Ihm sinne nach, und du begreifst genauer:
> Am farbigen Abglanz haben wir das Leben."

For Cusanus' commendation of this attitude, see Cassirer, *Individuum*, 45.

6. See his *Initia Doctrinae Physicae* (Wittenberg, 1549), prefatory letter to Michael Meienburg; repr. *Opera* (Corpus Reformatorum), Carl Gottlieb Bretschneider ed., VII (Halle, 1840), col. 473: "Non enim propterea abiicienda est doctrina certa et utilis vitae de multis rebus, etiamsi multa ignoramus; ac sciamus vere dei voluntatem esse, ut in mundi opificio vestigia ipsius aspiciamus et res nobis utiles ad vitam tuendam eligamus, praeparemus etiam nos ad illam aeternam academiam, in qua integram physicen discemus, cum ideam mundi nobis architectus ipse monstrabit."

This is not an isolated statement of Melanchthon's; on the contrary, he emphasizes again and again various aspects of the conviction that man's function and duty on earth is constant striving toward fuller understanding, despite the fact that he will always err and fall short of perfect insight in this life. See, for instance, in the text of the *Initia* (*Opera*, XIII), col. 181, the paragraph beginning "Nequaquam igitur certitudo in universum tollenda est," col. 188, paragraph beginning "Sed verum est aviditatem humanae mentis quaerere primam causam," col. 189 f., the two paragraphs beginning "Tota natura rerum velut theatrum est humani ingenii," and col. 336, "Omnis vera agnitio rerum a Deo conditarum et ordinatarum est res bona. . . ." Also in his *Liber de Anima* (rev. ed., Wittenberg, 1553; *Opera* XIII), he expresses similar sentiments repeatedly. See esp. col. 137, "Etsi penetrari acie humanae mentis rerum natura non potest, tamen vult Deus eam ab hominibus aspici, ut in ea consideremus testimonia de ipso, quae ostendunt et esse Deum, et qualis sit." And col. 143: "Ens quam late patet, hoc est, Deus et tota rerum universitas est obiectum intellectus, ad cuius agnitionem conditi sumus. . . . Et fuit haec lux ante naturae humanae depravationem illustrior, postea caligo secuta est, quare Deum et spirituales naturas et corporum substantiam minus intelligimus, sed utcunque eas a posteriori ratiocinando agnoscimus obscure et tenuiter."

7. Biedermann IV, 374 (June 6, 1831): *Faust*, lines 11936-37:

"Wer immer strebend sich bemüht,
Den können wir erlösen."

". . . in Faust selber eine immer höhere und reinere Tätigkeit bis ans Ende, und von oben die ihm zu Hilfe kommende ewige Liebe."

8. Lines 12104-111:

"Alles Vergängliche
Ist nur ein Gleichnis;
Das Unzulängliche,
Hier wird's Ereignis;
Das Unbeschreibliche,
Hier ist es getan;
Das Ewig-Weibliche
Zieht uns hinan."

What I include in this paragraph is a very brief summary of some of the results of a special study, "The Place of the 'Eternal Womanly' in Goethe's *Faust* Drama," which I hope will appear soon.

9. Biedermann III, 394 f. (May 6, 1827), or Gräf 394 f.: "Die Deutschen sind übrigens wunderliche Leute! Sie machen sich durch ihre tiefen Gedanken und Ideen, die sie überall suchen und überall hineinlegen, das Leben schwerer als billig. Ei, so habt doch endlich einmal die Courage, euch den Eindrücken hinzugeben, euch ergötzen zu lassen, euch rühren zu lassen, euch erheben zu lassen, ja euch belehren und zu etwas Grossem entflammen und ermutigen zu lassen; aber denkt nur nicht immer, es wäre alles eitel, wenn es nicht irgend abstrakter Gedanke und Idee wäre!

"Da kommen sie und fragen, welche Idee ich in meinem Faust zu verkörpern gesucht. Als ob ich das selber wüsste und aussprechen könnte! Vom Himmel durch die Welt zur Hölle, das wäre zur Not etwas; aber das ist keine Idee, sondern Gang der Handlung. Und ferner, dass der Teufel die Wette verliert, und dass ein aus schweren Verirrungen immerfort zum Bessern aufstrebender Mensch zu erlösen sei, das ist zwar ein wirksamer, manches erklärender guter Gedanke, aber es ist keine Idee, die dem Ganzen und jeder einzelnen Szene im besonderen zugrunde liege. Es hätte auch in der Tat ein schönes Ding werden müssen, wenn ich ein so reiches, buntes und so höchst mannigfaltiges Leben, wie ich es im Faust zur Anschauung gebracht, auf die magere Schnur einer einzigen durchgehenden Idee hätte reihen wollen!

"Es war im ganzen, fuhr Goethe fort, nicht meine Art, als Poet nach Verkörperung von etwas Abstraktem zu streben. Ich empfing in meinem Innern Eindrücke, und zwar Eindrücke sinn-

licher, lebensvoller, lieblicher, bunter hundertfältiger Art, wie eine
rege Einbildungskraft es mir darbot; und ich hatte als Poet weiter
nichts zu tun, als solche Anschauungen und Eindrücke in mir
künstlerisch zu runden und auszubilden und durch eine lebendige
Darstellung so zum Vorschein zu bringen, dass andere dieselbigen
Eindrücke erhielten, wenn sie mein Dargestelltes hörten oder
lasen.
"Wollte ich jedoch einmal als Poet irgendeine Idee darstellen,
so tat ich es in kleinen Gedichten. . . . Das einzige Produkt von
grösserem Umfang, wo ich mir bewusst bin, nach Darstellung
einer durchgreifenden Idee gearbeitet zu haben, wären etwa
meine Wahlverwandtschaften. Der Roman ist dadurch für den
Verstand fasslich geworden; aber ich will nicht sagen, dass er
dadurch besser geworden wäre! Vielmehr bin ich der Meinung:
je inkommensurabler und für den Verstand unfasslicher eine po-
etische Produktion, desto besser."

IX. CONCLUDING OBSERVATIONS

1. Biedermann II, 628 (April 13, 1823) and III, 189 (April 28,
1825). *W.A.* I, 28, 52: ". . . als ich in den Jünglingsjahren immer
mehr auf die Deutschheit des sechzehnten Jahrhunderts gewiesen
ward, so schloss ich gar bald auch die Franzosen jener herrlichen
Epoche in diese Neigung mit ein. Montaigne, Amyot, Rabelais,
Marot waren meine Freunde und erregten in mir Anteil und
Bewunderung." Cf. also *W.A.* I, 45, 171-177, esp. 173 f.
2. Biedermann I, 420-445.
3. See above ch. I, n. 2 and ch. VI, n. 36. It should be added that
the hitherto published works dealing with German literary and
intellectual influences upon other European countries during the
sixteenth and seventeenth centuries give only faint hints and fragmentary glimpses of the full panorama of interrelations. In the
field of German influences upon England, Charles H. Herford's
book on the sixteenth century was reasonably good for its day
(1886) though it should long ago have been superseded since
the amount of significant material which he does not include far
exceeds that which he includes. As for the book on the seventeenth
century by Gilbert Waterhouse (1914), it concentrates almost
exclusively on English influences upon Germany and claims that
there were practically none of importance in the opposite direc-

tion. My still incompleted catalogue of English seventeenth-century books and pamphlets that were reprints or translations of German books or were strongly under the influence of German thought and literature, comes to over one thousand numbers. And that excludes the trivia and ephemera. If even a partial and hasty listing were made of the volumes of poetry and of literary criticism by German Neo-Latin authors which were reprinted in Italy (and sometimes translated), a new attitude of respect for their contribution to the European Renaissance would inevitably result.

4. *W.A.* iv, 39, 216.

INDEX

aerial spirits, *see under* spirits
Aetna, 184
Agnello, Giovanni Battista, 175
Agrippa von Nettesheim, Henricus Cornelius, 29-30, 39, 55, 59, 154-155, 163
Alberti, Leon Battista, 40-41, 49
Albertus Magnus, 174
alchemy, *see under* occult
Alchimia Vera, 148, 175-176
Alethophilus, 166
Alexander Epicureus, 87-88, 174
Alexandrian philosophy, 88, 103
Allers, Rudolf, 144, 166, 171-172, 181-182, 185
Alrunes, 29
Amyot, Jacques, 125, 189
Anaximander, 166
Andreae, Johann Valentin, 30, 41, 68-69, 141, 147, 155
anima mundi, *see* spirit of the world
anima terrae, anima telluris, *see* Spirit of the Earth
anticipation, 10-11, 145
antiquarians and pedants, 19-22, 40, 106-107, 152; motif of manuscript, 20-21, 106; rhetorical tradition, 19-20, 22, 40, 151-152
antiquity, Greek and Roman, x, xii-xiii, 4, 7, 19-20, 28-30, 42, 49, 61, 65-66, 72, 75-76, 81-83, 88, 90-91, 101, 111, 124, 134, 149, 154, 174-175, 184-185
"Apocalypsis Spiritus Secreti," "The Apocalypse of the Secret Spirit," 88-89, 97, 175-176, and *see* Agnello
Apollo, Helios, 76, 80-81, 83, 87-88, 174-175
apotheosis, 48, 134, 144
Apuleius, Lucius, 154
Aratus, 84, 172
Archelaus, 167
Aretino, Pietro, 23
Aristophanes, 66, 167
Aristotle, 19, 57, 93
Arndt, Johann, 64
Arnold, E. Vernon, 144-145, 154, 166-167, 171-172, 181-182, 185
Arnold, Gottfried, 56

Asclepius, 134
astrology, *see under* occult
Athena, Minerva, Pallas, 83, 87, 174
Aurea Catena Homeri, 56, 62
Avicenna, 57, 89, 176

Bacon, Francis, 41, 161
Bacon, Roger, 142
Baroque, *see* seventeenth century
Bartscherer, Agnes, 7-8, 143, 147-148, 152, 155-156, 158, 163, 165-166, 169, 172, 175
Basilius Valentinus, 56, 80
Bayle, Pierre, 174
Beaumarchais, Pierre Augustin Caron de, 11
Behmen, *see* Boehme
Bekker, Balthasar, 166
Bernhard, Duke of Weimar, 11
Besold, Christoph, 68
Beutler, Ernst, 141
Beyer, Brother Albert, *see* "Colloqvivm . . ."
Bible, Biblical, Old and New Testament, 62, 78, 82, 99, 101, 113-116, 172, 181, 185-186
Biedermann, Flodoard Freiherr von, 144-146, 149, 154-156, 168, 171, 184, 187-189
Blake, William, 148
Blanchus, Vincentius, 93
Bodmer, Johann Jacob, 167
Boehme, Jacob, 148
Boerhaave, Hermann, 56
Boisserée, J. S. M. (Sulpiz), 159, 162
Book of Nature, *see under* nature
"The Book of the Apocalypse of Hermes . . . ," *see* "Apocalypsis . . ."
Borri, Giuseppe Francesco, 30
Bovillus, Carolus, 146
Boyd, James, 156
Brucker, Jacob, 63, 82, 165-166
Brühl, Carl Friedrich Moritz Paul, Graf von, 172
Bruno, Giordano, 41, 50-51, 62, 76, 70, 126, 160-161
Bry, Johannes Theodorus de, 64
Buchan, John, 71

191

INDEX

Date Due